Make Life Easier!

Your new best friend, the slow cooker, offers all kinds of help for busy, hassled, over-worked and over committed people. If you're one of these fun-loving people who wants out of the kitchen, but still wants home-cooked meals on the table, here's your answer.

Recipes are easy, use everyday ingredients and are family-tested and family-approved. You probably won't find recipes for fancy dinner parties in this cookbook, but you'll see some of the best every night, school-night or weekend night recipes you'll ever fix.

Recipes are favorite ones families grow up on and ones we remember long after adulthood. They are recipes that give you a warm and fuzzy feeling and let you know someone cares about you.

When you have home-cooked meals, you're giving your family a lifetime of memories and a never-ending bond.

Contents

*Statistical studies find that family
meals play a significant role in
childhood development. Children who
eat with their families four or more nights
per week are healthier, make better grades,
score higher on aptitude tests and are less
likely to have problems with drugs.*

Appetizers and Sandwiches

Nutty Crispy Snacks

3 cups Corn Chex® cereal
3 cups Quaker® oat squares
4 cups Crispix® cereal
2 cups pretzel sticks
1 cup salted peanuts
1 (16 ounce) can cashews
1 teaspoon seasoned salt
1 teaspoon garlic salt
1 teaspoon celery salt
¾ cup (1½ sticks) butter, melted

■ Place cereals, pretzel sticks, peanuts and
   cashews in sprayed slow cooker and sprinkle
   with seasoned salt, garlic salt and celery salt.
   Drizzle mixture with melted butter and
   gently toss.

■ Cover and cook on LOW for 3 to 4 hours.
   Uncover last 45 minutes. Yields 2 quarts.

*TIP: You may mix and match other cereals in the same
      amounts.*

Lazy Daisy Broccoli Dip

¾ cup (1½ sticks) butter
2 cups thinly sliced celery
1 onion, finely chopped
3 tablespoons flour
1 (10 ounce) can cream of chicken soup
1 (10 ounce) box chopped broccoli, thawed
1 (5 ounce) garlic cheese roll, cut in chunks
Wheat crackers or corn chips

- Melt butter in skillet and saute celery and onion, but do not brown; stir in flour. Pour into sprayed small slow cooker, stir in remaining ingredients and mix well.

- Cover and cook on LOW for 2 to 3 hours and stir several times. Serve with wheat crackers or corn chips. Serves 6 to 8.

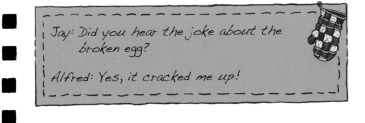

Jay: Did you hear the joke about the broken egg?

Alfred: Yes, it cracked me up!

Spinach-Artichoke Favorite

1 (16 ounce) package frozen chopped
    spinach, thawed
1 (14 ounce) can quartered artichoke hearts,
    drained, chopped
¾ cup mayonnaise
1½ cups shredded mozzarella cheese
1 teaspoon seasoned salt
Baguette chips or crackers

- Squeeze spinach between paper towels to
  remove excess moisture and place in sprayed
  slow cooker.

- Stir in artichoke hearts, mayonnaise, cheese,
  seasoned salt and a little pepper.

- Cover and cook on LOW for 1 hour 30 minutes
  to 2 hours. Keep on LOW while serving or
  for as long as 3 to 4 hours. Serve with chips or
  crackers. Yields 3 cups.

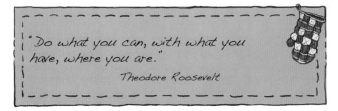

"Do what you can, with what you
have, where you are."

           Theodore Roosevelt

Unbelievable Crab Dip

2 (6 ounce) cans white crabmeat, drained, flaked
1 (8 ounce) package cream cheese, softened
½ cup (1 stick) butter, sliced
2 tablespoons white cooking wine
Chips or crackers

■ Combine crabmeat, cream cheese, butter and
   wine in sprayed, small slow cooker.

■ Cover and cook on LOW for 1 hour and gently
   stir to combine all ingredients. Serve from
   cooker with chips or crackers. Serves 4 to 6.

Slow cookers usually have two
temperature settings: LOW is about
200° and HIGH is about 300°. When
the heating elements are in the sides, food
is cooked on all sides and does not have
to be stirred. When the heating element is
in the bottom, it is best to stir the food
once or twice. Increase cooking time by 15
to 20 minutes each time the lid is removed.

Chicken-Enchilada Dip

2 pounds boneless, skinless chicken thighs, cubed
1 (10 ounce) can enchilada sauce
1 (7 ounce) can diced green chilies, drained
1 small onion, finely chopped
1 large red bell pepper, seeded, finely chopped
2 (8 ounce) packages cream cheese, cubed
1 (16 ounce) package shredded American cheese
Tortilla chips

- Place chicken, enchilada sauce, green chilies, onion and bell pepper in sprayed slow cooker.

- Cover and cook on LOW for 4 to 6 hours.

- Stir in cream cheese and American cheese and cook for additional 30 minutes. Stir several times during cooking. Serve with tortilla chips. Serves 8 to 10.

Honey Wings

16 - 18 chicken wings (about 3 pounds)
2 cups honey
1 cup barbecue sauce
1 teaspoon minced garlic
¼ cup soy sauce
¼ cup canola oil

- Cut off and discard wing tips and cut each wing at joint to make two sections. Sprinkle wings with a little salt and pepper and place on broiler pan.

- Broil for about 10 minutes; turn wings and broil for additional 10 minutes. Place wings in sprayed slow cooker.

- Combine honey, barbecue sauce, garlic, soy sauce and oil in bowl and mix. Pour mixture over wings. Cover and cook on LOW for 2 to 3 hours. Yields 32 to 36 wings.

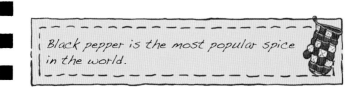

Black pepper is the most popular spice in the world.

Sweet and Sour Meatball Bites

1 (10 ounce) jar sweet and sour sauce
1/3 cup packed brown sugar
1/4 cup soy sauce
1 teaspoon garlic powder
1 (28 ounce) package frozen cooked meatballs,
    thawed
1 (20 ounce) can pineapple chunks, drained

Combine all ingredients in sprayed slow
cooker and mix well. Cover and cook on LOW
for 5 to 6 hours; stir occasionally. Serves 6.

*TIP: This can be served as an appetizer or served over
    seasoned spaghetti.*

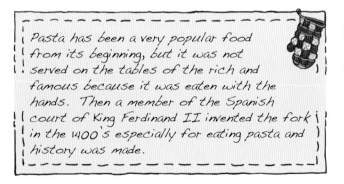

Pasta has been a very popular food
from its beginning, but it was not
served on the tables of the rich and
famous because it was eaten with the
hands. Then a member of the Spanish
court of King Ferdinand II invented the fork
in the 1400's especially for eating pasta and
history was made.

Hot Western-Style Sandwiches

3 pounds boneless chuck roast
¼ cup ketchup
2 teaspoons dijon-style mustard
¼ cup packed brown sugar
1 tablespoon Worcestershire sauce
½ teaspoon liquid smoke
French rolls or hamburger buns

▣ Place roast in sprayed slow cooker.

▣ Combine ketchup, mustard, brown sugar,
Worcestershire, liquid smoke and ½ teaspoon
salt and a little pepper in bowl. Pour mixture
over roast. Cover and cook on LOW for 8 to
9 hours.

▣ Remove roast and place on cutting board
and shred using 2 forks. Place in warm bowl
and add about 1 cup sauce from slow cooker.
Spoon shredded roast-sauce mixture onto
warmed (or toasted) rolls or buns. Yields
10 to 12 sandwiches.

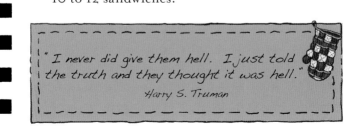

"I never did give them hell. I just told
the truth and they thought it was hell."
Harry S. Truman

Hot Open-Face Turkey Sandwiches

1 (2 pound) package turkey breast tenderloins
2 (12 ounce each) jars roasted turkey gravy
1 (28 ounce) package frozen home-style
    mashed potatoes
½ teaspoon poultry seasoning
1 teaspoon Worcestershire sauce
6 slices white or whole wheat bread, toasted
Paprika

▢ Place turkey in sprayed slow cooker and
   sprinkle with a little pepper. Pour gravy
   over top of turkey. Cover and cook on LOW
   for 8 to 10 hours.

▢ About 10 minutes before serving, prepare
   potatoes according to package directions.
   Remove turkey from cooker and cut into
   thin slices. Stir poultry seasoning and
   Worcestershire sauce into gravy in cooker.

▢ Place 2 slices turkey on each toasted slice of
   bread; top with ¼ cup mashed potatoes and
   spoon gravy over potatoes. Sprinkle with
   paprika. Yields 6 sandwiches.

*TIP: You can use 4 cups instant mashed potatoes instead of
    frozen mashed potatoes.*

Super Bowl Party Sandwiches

3 pounds boneless, skinless chicken thighs
2 tablespoons Caribbean jerk seasoning
1 (10 ounce) package frozen chopped bell peppers
    and onions, thawed
⅔ cup chicken broth
¼ cup ketchup
⅓ cup packed brown sugar
8 hoagie buns, split

■ Rub chicken thighs with jerk seasoning and a
little pepper. Place in sprayed slow cooker and
add bell peppers and onions.

■ Combine broth, ketchup and brown sugar in
bowl and pour over chicken. Cover and cook
on LOW for 6 to 8 hours.

■ Remove chicken from cooker with slotted
spoon and shred chicken using 2 forks.

■ Return chicken to slow cooker and mix
well. Fill buns with chicken mixture.
Yields 8 sandwiches.

Beer Brat Bites

3 - 6 (12 ounce) bottles favorite beer
Bratwurst
Onions, sliced
1 teaspoon cracked black pepper
Red pepper flakes
Buns
Mustard

 Grill brats over hot fire to get good grill marks
on brats. Saute onions in skillet and place in
sprayed slow cooker.

Place brats over onions in slow cooker and
pour enough beer over brats and onions to
cover. Add cracked black pepper and red
pepper flakes to taste.

Cover and cook on HIGH for several hours
until brats are thoroughly hot and soak up
some of the flavors. Serve with warm buns,
mustard, onions and ice-cold beer.

Soups and Stews

Ultimate Cheddar Cheese Soup

1 onion, finely chopped
1 red bell pepper, seeded, finely chopped
½ cup (1 stick) butter, melted
1 (16 ounce) package shredded extra sharp
    cheddar cheese
1 cup finely grated carrots
1 (14 ounce) can chicken broth
½ teaspoon minced garlic
2 tablespoons cornstarch
1 (1 pint) carton half-and-half cream

 Combine onion, bell pepper, butter, cheese,
    carrots, broth, garlic and a little pepper in
    sprayed slow cooker. Cover and cook on LOW
    for 5 to 7 hours.

Mix cornstarch with about 2 tablespoons
    half-and-half cream in bowl until mixture is
    smooth; stir in remaining cream.

Stir in cream mixture in slow cooker, cover
    and cook for additional 15 to 20 minutes or
    until soup is thoroughly hot. Serves 6.

*TIP: Top with a little shredded mozzarella cheese for an
    interesting presentation.*

Hearty Broccoli-Potato Soup

3 (14 ounce) cans chicken broth
3 ribs celery, sliced
1 onion, finely chopped
1 medium potato, peeled, chopped
1 (16 ounce) package frozen chopped
        broccoli, thawed
1 (1 pint) carton half-and-half cream
1 (5 ounce) package grated parmesan cheese

- Combine broth, celery, onion, potato,
  broccoli, half-and-half cream and 1 teaspoon
  salt in sprayed slow cooker. Cover and cook on
  LOW for 6 to 8 hours.

- Spoon soup in individual soup bowls and top
  with a little parmesan cheese. Serves 6.

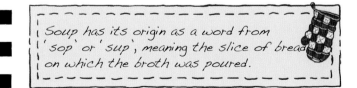

Soup has its origin as a word from
'sop' or 'sup', meaning the slice of bread
on which the broth was poured.

Quick-and-Easy French Onion Soup

¼ cup (½ stick) butter
3 large onions, sliced
3 (14 ounce) cans beef broth
1 teaspoon Worcestershire sauce
½ cup dry white wine
Butter, softened
8 thick slices French bread, toasted
1 cup grated gruyere or parmesan cheese

- Melt butter in skillet over medium heat. Stir in onions and cook for about 15 minutes or until onions are soft and very light brown.

- Place onions in sprayed slow cooker and add broth, Worcestershire and wine. Cover and cook on LOW for 4 to 4 hours 30 minutes.

- Spread light layer of butter on each slice of toasted bread. Ladle soup into 4 individual ovenproof bowls; top with slices of toasted bread and cheese; and place in oven at 400° to melt cheese. Serves 4.

Cheesy Bacon-Potato Soup

3½ pounds red potatoes, cubed
1 onion, chopped
1 (32 ounce) carton chicken broth
1 pint half-and-half cream
1 (8 ounce) package shredded cheddar cheese
1 (4 ounce) package prepared bacon bits

 Place potatoes and onions in sprayed slow
cooker. Combine broth, 1 teaspoon each of
salt and pepper; add to slow cooker. Cover
and cook on HIGH for 3 to 4 hours.

 Mash mixture and add half-and-half cream.
Cover and cook for additional 20 minutes.
Top each serving with cheese and bacon bits.
Serves 6.

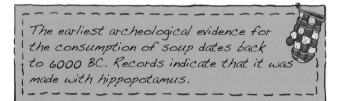

*The earliest archeological evidence for
the consumption of soup dates back
to 6000 BC. Records indicate that it was
made with hippopotamus.*

Summertime Zucchini Soup

1 small onion, very finely chopped
$3\frac{1}{2}$ – 4 cups grated zucchini with peels
2 (14 ounce) cans chicken broth
1 teaspoon seasoned salt
1 teaspoon dried dill weed
2 tablespoons butter, melted
1 (8 ounce) carton sour cream

- Combine all ingredients except sour cream with a little pepper in sprayed small slow cooker.

- Cover and cook on LOW for 2 hours. Fold in sour cream, cover and cook for about 10 minutes or just until soup is hot. Serves 4.

The Lone Ranger comes into town on a hot, dry day and gets off his horse. He tells Tonto to get his saddle blanket and wave it up and down while running around the horses to keep them cool. The Lone Ranger goes into the general store for supplies. Soon a big burly man comes into the store and says, "Is that your white horse out there?" "Yes, it is," said the Lone Ranger. The man said, "Did ya know ya left yur injun runnin'?"

Busy Bean-Barley Bounty

2 (15 ounce) cans pinto beans with liquid
3 (14 ounce) cans chicken broth
½ cup quick-cooking barley
1 (15 ounce) can Italian stewed tomatoes

- Combine beans, broth, barley, stewed tomatoes and ½ teaspoon pepper in sprayed slow cooker and stir well.

- Cover and cook on LOW for 4 to 5 hours. Serves 6 to 8.

Banzo Garbanzo Bowl

1 (16 ounce) package frozen chopped bell peppers and onions, thawed
1 pound Italian sausage, cut up
2 (14 ounce) cans beef broth
1 (15 ounce) can Italian stewed tomatoes
2 (15 ounce) can garbanzo beans, rinsed, drained

- Combine bell peppers and onions, sausage, broth, tomatoes, beans and ½ teaspoon salt in sprayed slow cooker. Cover and cook on LOW for 4 to 6 hours. Serves 6.

Creamy Tomato Soup

2 (28 ounce) cans diced tomatoes
¼ cup (½ stick) butter, melted
2 tablespoons brown sugar
2 tablespoons tomato paste
2 tablespoons flour
1 (14 ounce) can chicken broth
1 (8 ounce) carton whipping cream

- Drain tomatoes (reserving liquid) and place in blender; puree tomatoes and pour into sprayed slow cooker. Add reserved liquid, butter, brown sugar, tomato paste and ½ teaspoon salt.

- Mix flour with about ½ cup broth in bowl until mixture is smooth and stir in remaining broth. Add flour-broth mixture to cooker. Cover and cook on LOW for 6 to 8 hours.

- Stir in cream, cover and cook for additional 20 minutes or until soup is thoroughly hot. Serves 6.

Screwy Rotini-Veggie Soup

1 (32 ounce) carton chicken broth
1 (12 ounce) can tomato juice
2 carrots, peeled, sliced
3 ribs celery, chopped
1 onion, chopped
1 (15 ounce) can stewed tomatoes
1 teaspoon dried basil
1 (10 ounce) package frozen green peas, thawed
1 (8 ounce) package whole wheat rotini
    (corkscrew) pasta

■ Combine broth, juice, carrots, celery, onion,
tomatoes, basil and a little salt and pepper in
sprayed slow cooker. Cover and cook on LOW
for 8 to 9 hours.

■ Increase heat to HIGH and stir in peas and pasta.
Cover and cook for additional 15 to 20 minutes
or until pasta is tender. Serves 8 to 10.

Before tomatoes were brought to Europe
from the Americas, pasta was generally
eaten with seasoning or cheese. Tomatoes
revolutionized pasta. Italy had an ideal growing
climate for tomatoes. Tomato sauces were
popular with pasta by the early 1800's.

One-Pot Meal

1½ pounds lean ground beef
1 teaspoon seasoned salt
1 (32 ounce) carton beef broth
2 (15 ounce) cans stewed tomatoes
1 (15 ounce) can pinto beans, rinsed, drained
2 ribs celery, sliced
1 (8 ounce) can sliced carrots
1 cup macaroni, cooked, drained
1 cup shredded cheddar cheese

- Crumble beef into sprayed slow cooker and
  add seasoned salt, broth, tomatoes, beans,
  celery and carrots.

- Cover and cook on LOW for 6 to 8 hours.
  Increase heat to HIGH, add cooked macaroni
  and cook for additional 15 minutes. Sprinkle
  a heaping tablespoon cheese over each
  individual serving. Serves 6.

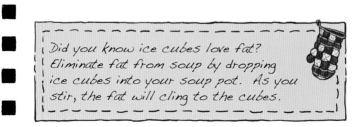

Did you know ice cubes love fat?
Eliminate fat from soup by dropping
ice cubes into your soup pot. As you
stir, the fat will cling to the cubes.

Hearty Italian Vegetable Soup

1 pound lean ground beef
2 teaspoons minced garlic
1 green bell pepper, seeded, chopped
3 (14 ounce) cans beef broth
1 (15 ounce) can stewed tomatoes
2 (15 ounce) can cannellini beans, rinsed, drained
1 teaspoon Italian seasoning
2 medium zucchini, sliced
1 (10 ounce) package frozen chopped spinach,
    thawed

Brown ground beef in skillet, drain and
combine with garlic, bell pepper, broth,
tomatoes, beans and Italian seasoning in
sprayed slow cooker. Cover and cook on LOW
for 5 to 7 hours.

Stir in zucchini and chopped spinach and cook
for additional 1 hour. Serves 6 to 8.

TIP: *If you have pasta in the pantry, add it to the pot. You
can put just about anything in this soup.*

Amigos Taco Soup Olé

1½ pounds lean ground beef
2 (15 ounce) cans chili beans with liquid
1 (15 ounce) can whole kernel corn with liquid
2 (15 ounce) cans stewed tomatoes
1 (10 ounce) can diced tomatoes and green chilies
1 (.04 ounce) packet ranch dressing mix
1 (1 ounce) packet taco seasoning
Shredded cheddar cheese

▨ Brown ground beef in large skillet, drain and transfer to sprayed slow cooker.

▨ Add remaining ingredients and stir well. Cover and cook on LOW for 8 to 10 hours. When serving, sprinkle cheese over each serving. Serve 6 to 8.

Beef and Black Bean Soup

1 pound lean ground beef
2 onions, chopped
2 cups sliced celery
2 (14 ounce) cans beef broth
1 (15 ounce) can Mexican stewed tomatoes
2 (15 ounce) cans black beans, rinsed, drained

 Brown beef in skillet until no longer pink.
Place in sprayed slow cooker.

Add onions, celery, broth, tomatoes,
black beans, ¾ cup water plus a little salt
and pepper. Cover and cook on LOW for
6 to 7 hours or on HIGH for 3 hours to
3 hours 30 minutes. Serves 6 to 8.

TIP: If you like a zestier soup, add 1 teaspoon chili powder.

Beef and Barley Soup

1 pound lean ground beef
3 (14 ounce) cans beef broth
¾ cup quick-cooking barley
3 cups sliced carrots
2 cups sliced celery
2 teaspoons beef seasoning

- Brown ground beef in skillet, drain and transfer to sprayed slow cooker.

- Add beef broth, barley, carrots, celery and beef seasoning. Cover and cook on LOW for 7 to 8 hours. Serves 4.

Beefy Rice Soup

1 pound lean beef stew meat
1 (14 ounce) can beef broth
1 (7 ounce) box beef-flavored rice and vermicelli mix
1 (10 ounce) package frozen peas and carrots
2½ cups vegetable juice

- Sprinkle stew meat with seasoned pepper, brown in non-stick skillet, drain and place in sprayed, large slow cooker.

- Add broth, rice and vermicelli mix, peas and carrots, vegetable juice and 2 cups water. Cover and cook on LOW for 6 to 7 hours. Serves 4 to 6.

Select Beef-Potato Soup

2 (14 ounce) cans beef broth
1 (10 ounce) can cream of celery soup
1 cup half-and-half cream
1 pound boneless beef chuck, cut into 1-inch pieces
1 (5 ounce) box au gratin potato mix
½ teaspoon dried thyme
1 (15 ounce) can green peas, drained
Grated parmesan cheese

■ Pour beef broth and cream of celery soup into
slow cooker and whisk well. Place beef pieces,
potato mix, thyme, 2 cups water in sprayed
slow cooker.

■ Cover and cook on LOW for 7 to 8 hours or on
HIGH for 3 hours 30 minutes to 4 hours.

■ (If cooking on HIGH, reduce heat to LOW.)
Stir in half-and-half cream and peas; cover
and cook for additional 15 to 20 minutes.
Sprinkle parmesan cheese over each serving.
Serves 4 to 5.

All-American Soup

3 boneless, skinless chicken breast halves, cut
    into strips
1 onion, chopped
1 (10 ounce) can diced tomatoes and green chilies
2 large baking potatoes, peeled, cubed
2 (14 ounce) cans chicken broth
1 (10 ounce) can cream of celery soup
1 cup milk
1 teaspoon dried basil
1 (8 ounce) package shredded Velveeta® cheese
½ cup sour cream

■ Place chicken strips, onion, tomatoes and
green chilies, potatoes, milk and basil in
sprayed slow cooker. Heat broth and soup in
saucepan to thin and pour over vegetables.

■ Cover and cook on LOW for 6 to 8 hours.

■ Stir in cheese and sour cream. Cover and
cook for additional 10 to 15 minutes or just
until cheese melts. Serves 6 to 8.

*TIP: You can leave out the 2 cans of broth and serve this
chicken dish over hot cooked rice topped with about
1 cup of lightly crushed potato chips.*

Knockout Minestrone

1 (15 ounce) can cannellini beans, rinsed, drained
1 (15 ounce) can pinto beans, drained
1 (15 ounce) can kidney beans, rinsed, drained
2 (15 ounce) cans Italian stewed tomatoes with liquid
1 pound boneless beef chuck, cut in ½-inch pieces
1 cup peeled, shredded carrots
1 cup dried favorite pasta
1 medium zucchini, sliced
Parmesan cheese

■ Combine beans, stewed tomatoes, beef,
   carrots and a little salt and pepper in sprayed
   slow cooker. Cover and cook on LOW for
   8 to 9 hours or on HIGH for 4 hours to
   4 hours 30 minutes.

■ Add pasta and zucchini and cook on HIGH
   heat for 30 to 45 minutes. Sprinkle each
   serving with a little parmesan cheese.
   Serves 8.

Old-Time Chicken Soup

6 boneless, skinless chicken thighs, cut into
    1-inch pieces
3 (14 ounce) cans chicken broth
1 carrot, sliced
2 ribs celery, sliced
1 onion, chopped
1 (15 ounce) can stewed tomatoes
1 (8 ounce) can green peas, drained
1 teaspoon dried thyme
½ cup elbow macaroni

- Combine chicken pieces, broth, carrot, celery,
  onion, tomatoes, peas, thyme and 1 teaspoon
  each of salt and pepper in sprayed slow cooker.

- Cover and cook on LOW for 6 hours 30 minutes
  to 7 hours.

- Increase heat to HIGH, add macaroni, cover and
  cook for additional 30 minutes. Serves 6.

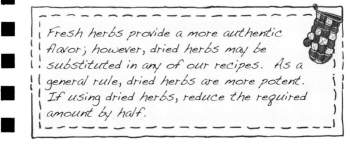

Fresh herbs provide a more authentic flavor; however, dried herbs may be substituted in any of our recipes. As a general rule, dried herbs are more potent. If using dried herbs, reduce the required amount by half.

Curly Noodle Soup

6 - 7 boneless, skinless chicken thighs
1 (16 ounce) package baby carrots, halved
1 (8 ounce) can sliced bamboo shoots, drained
1 (8 ounce) can sliced water chestnuts, drained
1 (3 ounce) package Oriental-flavor ramen noodle
    soup mix
1 (32 ounce) carton chicken broth
2 tablespoons butter, melted
1 (10 ounce) package frozen green peas,
    thawed, drained

▨ Layer chicken thighs, carrots, bamboo shoots,
water chestnuts, seasoning packet from noodles,
broth and butter in sprayed slow cooker. Cover
and cook on LOW for 7 to 8 hours.

▨ Remove chicken thighs with slotted spoon and
shred with 2 forks. Return chicken to slow
cooker and add peas and noodles; cover and
cook for additional 10 minutes or until noodles
are tender. Serves 6.

Chicken-Barley Soup

1½ - 2 pounds boneless, skinless chicken thighs
1 (16 ounce) package frozen stew vegetables
1 (1 ounce) packet dry vegetable soup mix
1¼ cups pearl barley
3 (14 ounce) cans chicken broth

Combine all ingredients with 1 teaspoon each
of salt and pepper and 4 cups water in large,
sprayed slow cooker.

Cover and cook on LOW for 5 to 6 hours or
on HIGH for 3 hours. Serves 6 to 8.

Lucky Chicken Soup

3 cups cooked, cubed chicken
1 (15 ounce) can stewed tomatoes
1 (10 ounce) can enchilada sauce
1 onion, chopped
1 teaspoon minced garlic
1 (14 ounce) can chicken broth
1 (15 ounce) can whole kernel corn
1 teaspoon chili powder

Combine chicken, tomatoes, enchilada sauce,
onion, garlic, broth, corn, chili powder and
2 cups water in sprayed slow cooker. Cover
and cook on LOW for 6 to 8 hours or on
HIGH for 3 to 4 hours. Serves 8.

Chicken-Veggie Surprise

3 (14 ounce) can chicken broth
1 (15 ounce) can sliced carrots, drained
1 (15 ounce) can green peas, drained
1 red bell pepper, seeded, chopped
1 teaspoon dried tarragon
2 cups cooked, cubed chicken
1 (16 ounce) package frozen broccoli florets
4 ounces thin egg noodles

- Combine broth, carrots, peas, bell pepper, tarragon, chicken and broccoli in sprayed slow cooker. Cover and cook on LOW for 5 to 7 hours.

- Stir in noodles, cover and cook for additional 1 hour. Serves 6 to 8.

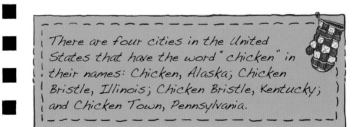

There are four cities in the United States that have the word "chicken" in their names: Chicken, Alaska; Chicken Bristle, Illinois; Chicken Bristle, Kentucky; and Chicken Town, Pennsylvania.

Turkey and Mushroom Soup

A great way to use leftover chicken or turkey

2 cups sliced shitake or sliced button mushrooms
2 ribs celery, sliced
1 small onion, chopped
2 tablespoons butter
1 (15 ounce) can sliced carrots
2 (14 ounce) cans chicken broth
½ cup orzo pasta
2 cups cooked, chopped turkey

Saute mushrooms, celery and onion in butter in skillet until onions are translucent.

Transfer vegetables to sprayed slow cooker and add carrots, broth, orzo and turkey. (Do not use smoked turkey.) Cover and cook on LOW for 2 to 3 hours or on HIGH for 1 to 2 hours. Serves 4 to 6.

TIP: Make a main dish by omitting 1 can chicken broth and adding 1 cup turkey. Place in a casserole dish and sprinkle with slivered almonds. Bake at 350° for about 10 to 15 minutes.

Corny Turkey Soup

1 onion, chopped
1 red bell pepper, seeded, chopped
1 (15 ounce) can cream-style corn
1 (15 ounce) can whole kernel corn
2 (14 ounce) cans chicken broth
1 cup whipping cream
2 - 3 cups cooked, cubed turkey
4 green onions, sliced

- Combine onion, bell pepper, cream-style corn, whole kernel corn, broth, cream and cubed turkey in sprayed slow cooker.

- Cover and cook on LOW for 5 to 7 hours. Scatter a few sliced green onions over each serving. Serves 4 to 6.

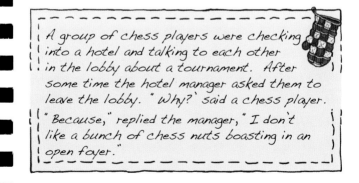

A group of chess players were checking into a hotel and talking to each other in the lobby about a tournament. After some time the hotel manager asked them to leave the lobby. "Why?" said a chess player.

"Because," replied the manager, "I don't like a bunch of chess nuts boasting in an open foyer."

Turkey and Rice Soup

1 (10 ounce) package frozen chopped bell peppers
and onions, thawed
¼ cup (½ stick) butter, melted
2 (14 ounce) cans turkey or chicken broth
1 (6 ounce) box roasted garlic long grain–wild rice
mix
2 cups cooked, diced turkey
2 (10 ounce) cans cream of chicken soup
1 cup milk
1 (8 ounce) can green peas, drained

Combine bell peppers and onions, butter,
turkey broth, rice and turkey in sprayed slow
cooker.

Heat cream of chicken soup and milk in
saucepan over low heat. Stir out lumps and
pour over turkey.

Cover and cook on LOW for 6 to 8 hours.
One hour before serving, add peas. Serves 6.

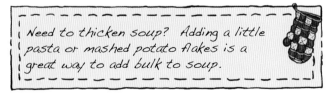

Need to thicken soup? Adding a little
pasta or mashed potato flakes is a
great way to add bulk to soup.

Lucky Black-Eyed Pea Soup

1 onion, chopped
2 cups cooked, cubed ham
2 (15 ounce) cans black-eyed peas with jalapenos
    with liquid
2 ribs celery, sliced
1 (14 ounce) can chicken broth
1 teaspoon minced garlic
1 teaspoon dried sage

Combine all ingredients in sprayed slow
cooker. Cover and cook on LOW for 5 to
7 hours. Serves 4.

Florentine-Style Soup

3 - 4 large potatoes, peeled, diced
I onion, finely diced
I (I pound) ham hock
I (32 ounce) carton chicken broth
I½ teaspoons seasoned salt
½ teaspoon dry mustard
I (10 ounce) package frozen chopped spinach,
    thawed, well drained*
I cup shredded cheddar or Swiss cheese

- Combine potatoes, onion, ham hock (or
  2 cups diced ham), broth, seasoned salt, a little
  pepper and mustard in sprayed slow cooker.
  Cover and cook on LOW for 7 to 8 hours.

- Remove ham hock, chop meat and discard
  bone; return meat to slow cooker. Increase
  heat to HIGH; add spinach; cover and cook
  for additional 20 minutes. Add cheese and
  stir until it melts. Serves 4 to 6.

*TIP: *Squeeze spinach between paper towels to remove
    excess moisture.*

If you don't like black specks in your
soup, try white pepper.

Tomato and White Bean Soup

- 1 (10 ounce) package frozen chopped bell peppers and onions, thawed
- 1 (15 ounce) can diced tomatoes
- 2 (14 ounce) cans chicken broth
- 2 (15 ounce) cans navy beans, rinsed, drained
- 1½ cups cooked, diced ham
- ½ cup chopped fresh parsley

  Combine all ingredients in sprayed slow
  cooker. Cover and cook on LOW for 5 to
  7 hours. Serves 4

Blue Ribbon Beef Stew

I (2½ - 3 pound) beef chuck roast, cubed
2 (14 ounce) cans beef broth
I teaspoon dried thyme
2 teaspoons minced garlic
I pound new (red) potatoes, quartered
2 carrots, peeled, sliced
3 ribs celery, sliced
I (I ounce) packet onion soup mix
I (15 ounce) can green beans, drained

Combine cubed beef, broth, ¾ cup water,
thyme, garlic, potatoes, carrots, celery and
onion soup mix in sprayed slow cooker. Cover
and cook on LOW for 7 to 9 hours.

Stir in green beans, cover and let stand for
about 10 minutes. Serves 6 to 8.

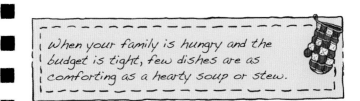

When your family is hungry and the budget is tight, few dishes are as comforting as a hearty soup or stew.

Easy Stroganoff Stew

1 (1 ounce) packet onion soup mix
2 (10 ounce) cans golden mushroom soup
2 pounds stew meat
1 onion, chopped
1 (4 ounce) can sliced mushrooms
1 (8 ounce) carton sour cream
1 (8 ounce) package wide noodles

■ Combine soup mix, soup and 2 soup cans
water in saucepan and heat to thin. Pour over
stew meat, onion and mushrooms in sprayed
slow cooker. Cover and cook on LOW for 7 to
9 hours.

■ Cook noodles according to package directions
and place on serving platter. Stir sour cream
into stew and spoon stew over noodles. Serves
6 to 8.

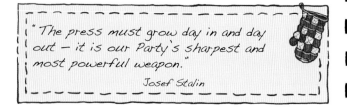

"The press must grow day in and day
out — it is our Party's sharpest and
most powerful weapon."

Josef Stalin

South-of-the Border Frijole Stew

1 pound lean ground beef, browned, drained
1 (15 ounce) can Mexican stewed tomatoes
1 (15 ounce) can pinto beans with liquid
1 onion, chopped
2 (10 ounce) cans enchilada sauce
1 (8 ounce) package shredded 4-cheese blend
Tortilla chips, optional

▨ Combine beef, tomatoes, beans, onion,
enchilada sauce and 1 cup water in sprayed slow
cooker and mix well. Cover and cook on LOW
for 6 to 8 hours or on HIGH for 3 to 4 hours.

▨ Stir in shredded cheese until it melts. If
desired, top each serving with a few crushed
tortilla chips. Serves 6 to 8.

Chicken and Lima Bean Stew

1½ pound boneless, skinless chicken thighs, cubed
1 (28 ounce) can diced tomatoes
1 (15 ounce) can baby lima beans, drained
1 (15 ounce) can whole kernel corn, drained
1 tablespoon chopped garlic
1 tablespoon ground cumin
1 tablespoon dried oregano
3 tablespoons Worcestershire sauce
¼ cup tomato paste

Place all ingredients in slow cooker and mix
well. Cover and cook on LOW 5 to 6 hours.
Serves 6.

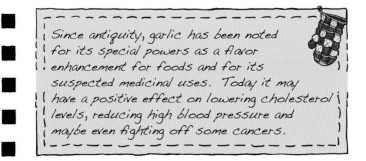

Since antiquity, garlic has been noted
for its special powers as a flavor
enhancement for foods and for its
suspected medicinal uses. Today it may
have a positive effect on lowering cholesterol
levels, reducing high blood pressure and
maybe even fighting off some cancers.

First-Class Vegetarian Chili

1 tablespoon canola oil
1 (16 ounce) package frozen chopped bell peppers
  and onions, thawed
1 teaspoon minced garlic
2 (15 ounce) cans stewed tomatoes
1 (15 ounce) can navy beans, rinsed, drained
1 (15 ounce) can kidney beans, rinsed, drained
1 (8 ounce) can whole kernel corn, drained
¼ cup tomato paste
2 teaspoons ground cumin
1 tablespoon chili powder

▣ Heat oil in skillet on medium-high heat and
  cook bell peppers and onions, and garlic for
  about 5 minutes, stirring often. Place mixture
  in sprayed slow cooker.

▣ Add tomatoes, beans, corn, tomato paste,
  cumin, chili powder and a little salt and
  pepper; mix well. Cover and cook on LOW
  for 4 to 5 hours. Serves 6.

White Chicken Chili

1½ pounds boneless, skinless chicken thighs
3 (15 ounce) cans great northern beans,
    rinsed, drained
1 (15 ounce) can white hominy, drained
1 (1 ounce) packet taco seasoning
1 (7 ounce) can diced green chilies
1 (10 ounce) can cream of chicken soup
1 (8 ounce) carton sour cream
Chopped green onions

- Place chicken in sprayed slow cooker and top
  with beans, hominy, taco seasoning and green
  chilies. Heat chicken soup in saucepan to thin
  and pour over chicken.

- Cover and cook on LOW for 8 to 10 hours.

- Before serving, stir vigorously to break up
  chicken pieces. Place 1 tablespoon sour cream
  and few pieces green onions on top of each
  serving. Serves 6.

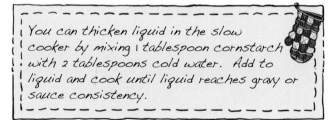

You can thicken liquid in the slow
cooker by mixing 1 tablespoon cornstarch
with 2 tablespoons cold water. Add to
liquid and cook until liquid reaches gravy or
sauce consistency.

Traditional Chili

2 pounds lean beef chili meat
1 large onion, finely chopped
1 (10 ounce) can diced tomatoes and green chilies
2½ cups tomato juice
2 tablespoons chili powder
1 tablespoon ground cumin
1 tablespoon minced garlic
1 (15 ounce) can pinto or kidney beans

Combine chili meat, onion, tomatoes and green chilies, tomato juice, chili powder, cumin, garlic and 1 cup water in sprayed large slow cooker and mix well. Cover and cook on LOW for 7 to 9 hours.

Add pinto or kidney beans, cover and cook for additional 30 minutes. Serves 4 to 6.

Handy Corn Chowder

2 medium potatoes, peeled, diced
1 (10 ounce) package frozen chopped bell peppers
    and onions, thawed
1 (15 ounce) can cream-style corn
1 (15 ounce) can whole kernel corn
1 (10 ounce) can cream of celery soup
1 teaspoon seasoned salt
2 tablespoons cornstarch
1 (14 ounce) can chicken broth, divided
1 (8 ounce) carton whipping cream

▪ Combine potatoes, bell pepper-onion
mixture, cream-style corn, corn, soup and
seasoned salt in sprayed slow cooker.

▪ In small bowl, combine cornstarch and about
¼ cup of the broth and stir until mixture is
smooth; stir in remaining broth and add to
slow cooker. Cover and cook on LOW heat for
6 to 8 hours.

▪ Stir in whipping cream; cover and cook
additional 15 to 20 minutes or until chowder
is thoroughly hot. Serves 6.

Succulent Crab Chowder

3 medium red potatoes, cut into ½-inch cubes
1 (16 ounce) package frozen corn, thawed
2 ribs celery, sliced
½ cup finely chopped red bell pepper
1 teaspoon dried thyme
1 (32 ounce) carton chicken broth
1 (8 ounce) carton whipping cream
⅓ cup cornstarch
2 (6 ounce) cans crabmeat, drained

Layer potatoes, corn, celery and bell pepper in
sprayed slow cooker. Sprinkle with thyme and
a little pepper. Stir in chicken broth, cover
and cook on LOW for 4 hours.

Combine cream and cornstarch in bowl and
slowly stir into slow cooker. Increase heat to
HIGH, cover and cook for 1 additional hour.
Stir in crabmeat and serve hot. Serves 4 to 6.

*I went to a seafood disco last week...
and pulled a mussel.*

Easy Oyster Stew

4 green onions, finely chopped
½ cup (1 stick) butter, melted
1 teaspoon Worcestershire sauce
2 (12 ounce) containers fresh oysters with liquid
1 (8 ounce) carton whipping cream
3 cups milk
Dash of cayenne pepper

⬛ Combine onions, butter and Worcestershire in
sprayed slow cooker. Cover and cook on LOW
for 2 hours or until mixture is hot.

⬛ Stir in oysters with liquid, cream, milk,
cayenne pepper and a little salt. Cover and
cook for about 30 minutes or until oyster
edges begin to curl and stew is thoroughly hot.
Serves 6.

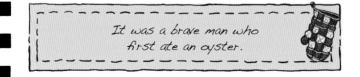

*It was a brave man who
first ate an oyster.*

Shrimp and Chicken Jambalaya

4 chicken breast halves, cubed
1 (28 ounce) can diced tomatoes
1 onion, chopped
1 green bell pepper, seeded, chopped
1 (14 ounce) can chicken broth
½ cup dry white wine or cooking wine
2 teaspoons dried oregano
2 teaspoons Cajun seasoning
½ teaspoon cayenne pepper
1 pound cooked, peeled, veined shrimp
2 cups cooked white rice

▧ Place all ingredients except shrimp and rice in
   sprayed slow cooker and stir. Cover and cook
   on LOW for 6 to 8 hours.

▧ Turn heat to HIGH, stir in shrimp and rice
   and cook for additional 15 to 20 minutes.
   Serves 4 to 6.

Rice came to the South by way of a storm-ravaged, merchant ship sailing from Madagascar and reaching the port of Charleston for safe haven. As a gift to the people, the ship's captain gave a local planter some "Golden Seed Rice" and by 1700, rice was a major crop in the colonies.

Vegetables and Side Dishes

Tomato-Artichoke Pasta

3 (15 ounce) cans Italian stewed tomatoes, divided
2 (14 ounce) cans artichoke hearts, drained,
    quartered
1 teaspoon minced garlic
1 (5 ounce) can evaporated milk
1 (12 ounce) package penne pasta
1 cup grated parmesan cheese

■ Drain 2 cans of tomatoes and place in sprayed
   slow cooker. Add tomatoes with liquid,
   artichoke hearts and garlic.

■ Cover and cook on LOW for 6 to 8 hours or
   on HIGH for 3 to 4 hours.

■ Stir in evaporated milk and let stand covered
   for about 10 minutes. Cook pasta according to
   package directions, drain and place on serving
   plate. Serve artichoke mixture over pasta and
   sprinkle each serving with a little parmesan
   cheese. Serves 6.

Thomas Jefferson raised tomatoes
in the 1780's and helped spread their
popularity.

Perfect Cinnamon Carrots

2 (16 ounce) packages baby carrots
¾ cup packed brown sugar
¼ cup honey
½ cup orange juice
2 tablespoons butter, melted
¾ teaspoon ground cinnamon

- Place carrots in sprayed slow cooker.

- Combine brown sugar, honey, orange juice, butter and cinnamon in bowl and mix well. Pour over carrots and stir to make sure sugar-cinnamon mixture coats carrots. Cover and cook on LOW for 3 hours 30 minutes to 4 hours and stir twice during cooking time.

- About 20 minutes before serving, use slotted spoon to transfer carrots to serving dish and cover to keep warm.

- Pour liquid from cooker into saucepan; boil for several minutes until liquid reduces by half. Spoon over carrots in serving dish. Serves 6 to 8.

Broccoli-Cheese Bake

¼ cup (½ stick) butter, melted
1 (10 ounce) can cream of mushroom soup
1 (10 ounce) can cream of onion soup
1 cup instant rice
1 (8 ounce) package cubed Velveeta® cheese
2 (10 ounce) packages frozen chopped
      broccoli, thawed

▢ Heat mushroom soup and onion soups in
   saucepan with ½ cup water to thin enough
   to pour it over ingredients.

▢ Combine all ingredients in sprayed slow
   cooker, pour soups over top and stir well.
   Cover and cook on HIGH for 2 to 3 hours.
   Serves 4 to 6.

Buttery Baked Corn

2 (15 ounce) cans whole kernel corn
2 (15 ounce) cans cream-style corn
½ cup (1 stick) butter, melted
1 (8 ounce) carton sour cream
1 (8 ounce) package jalapeno cornbread mix

▢ Combine all ingredients in large bowl and mix
   well. Pour into sprayed slow cooker, cover and
   cook on LOW for 4 to 5 hours. Serves 6 to 8.

Crunchy Green Bean Casserole

2 (16 ounce) packages frozen whole green
    beans, thawed
3 ribs celery, diagonally sliced
1 red bell pepper, julienned
2 (11 ounce) cans sliced water chestnuts, drained
½ cup slivered almonds
1 (10 ounce) can cream of chicken soup
1 (3 ounce) can french-fried onions

🔲 Combine green beans, celery, bell pepper,
    water chestnuts and almonds in sprayed slow
    cooker. Heat soup with about ¼ cup water to
    thin soup just enough so you can pour it over
    vegetable mixture.

🔲 Cover and cook on LOW for 2 to 4 hours.

🔲 About 10 minutes before serving, top with
    fried onions. Serves 6 to 8.

The Onion Solution

2 (10 ounce) bags frozen small whole onions, thawed
2 ribs celery, very thinly sliced
1 green bell pepper, seeded, chopped
¼ cup (½ stick) butter, melted
1 tablespoon red wine vinegar
2 tablespoons brown sugar
½ teaspoon seasoned salt

▪ Combine onions, celery, bell pepper, melted
butter, vinegar, brown sugar, seasoned salt and
pepper in bowl; toss to coat vegetables well.
Spoon into sprayed slow cooker.

▪ Cover and cook on LOW for 4 hours to
4 hours 30 minutes. Serves 6.

" I am only one, but I am one. I cannot
do everything, but I can do something.
And because I cannot do everything, I
will not refuse to do the something that
I can do. What I can do, I should do.
And what I should do, by the grace of
God, I will do."

Edward Everett Hale

Roasted New Potatoes

18 - 20 new (red) potatoes with peels
¼ cup (½ stick) butter, melted
1 tablespoon dried parsley
½ teaspoon garlic powder
½ teaspoon paprika

■ Combine all ingredients plus ½ teaspoon
each of salt and pepper in sprayed slow cooker
and mix well. Cover and cook on LOW for
7 hours or on HIGH for 3 hours 30 minutes
to 4 hours.

■ When ready to serve, remove potatoes with
slotted spoon to serving dish and cover to
keep warm.

■ Add about 2 tablespoons water to liquid in
cooker and stir until they blend well. Pour
mixture over potatoes. Serves 4 to 6.

Hasty Hash Browns

1 (32 ounce) package frozen hash-brown
    potatoes, thawed
1 (8 ounce) package shredded sharp cheddar cheese
1 (8 ounce) carton fresh whole mushrooms, sliced
1 (16 ounce) package frozen chopped bell peppers
    and onions, thawed
1 teaspoon seasoned salt
1 (10 ounce) can cream of mushroom soup

▨ Combine potatoes, cheese, mushrooms, bell
peppers and onions, and seasoned salt in
sprayed slow cooker. Heat soup with ¼ cup
water to thin and pour over potatoes.

▨ Cover and cook on LOW for 7 to 9 hours or
on HIGH for 4 hours. Stir gently before
serving. Serves 8.

*Slow cookers work best when filled to
between two-thirds and three-fourths
of capacity. Filling a cooker to the brim
will prevent even cooking and will require a
longer cooking time.*

Cheezy Potatoes

- 1 (28 ounce) bag frozen diced potatoes with onions
    and peppers, thawed
- 1 (8 ounce) package shredded Monterey Jack and
    cheddar cheese blend
- 1 (10 ounce) can cream of celery soup
- 1 (8 ounce) carton sour cream

Combine potatoes, cheese, soup, sour cream
and 1 teaspoon pepper in sprayed slow cooker
and mix well. Cover and cook on LOW 4 to
6 hours. Stir well before serving. Serves 6 to 8.

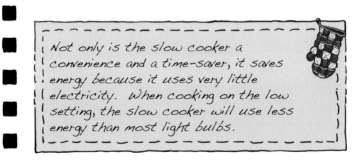

Not only is the slow cooker a convenience and a time-saver, it saves energy because it uses very little electricity. When cooking on the low setting, the slow cooker will use less energy than most light bulbs.

Thanksgiving Sweet Potatoes

2 (20 ounce) cans sweet potatoes, drained, mashed
½ cup (1 stick) plus ⅓ cup (⅔ stick) butter, divided
¼ cup sugar
¼ cup plus ⅓ cup packed brown sugar, divided
2 eggs, slightly beaten
½ cup milk
⅓ cup chopped pecans
3 tablespoons flour

■ Combine mashed sweet potatoes, ½ cup
melted butter, sugar and ¼ cup brown sugar
in large bowl and mix well. Stir in beaten eggs
and milk and spoon into sprayed slow cooker.

■ Combine remaining melted butter, pecans,
flour and remaining brown sugar in bowl and
sprinkle over sweet potato mixture. Cover and
cook on HIGH for 3 to 4 hours. Serves 8.

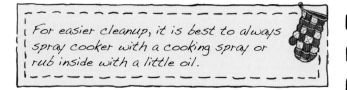

*For easier cleanup, it is best to always
spray cooker with a cooking spray or
rub inside with a little oil.*

Creamed Spinach

2 (10 ounce) packages frozen chopped spinach,
    thawed
1 (16 ounce) carton small curd cottage cheese
1½ cups shredded American or cheddar cheese
3 eggs, beaten
¼ cup (½ stick) butter, melted
¼ cup flour

■ Drain spinach and squeeze between paper
    towels to completely remove excess moisture.

■ Combine all ingredients in bowl and mix
    well. Spoon into sprayed slow cooker. Cover
    and cook on HIGH for 1 hour, reduce heat to
    LOW and cook for additional 3 to 5 hours or
    until knife inserted in center comes out clean.
    Serves 4 to 6.

*Families are like fudge... mostly sweet
with a few nuts.*

Spinach-Artichoke Special

2 (16 ounce) packages frozen chopped spinach,
    thawed, drained
1 onion, chopped
1 red bell pepper, seeded, chopped
¼ cup (½ stick) butter, melted
1 cup shredded Italian cheese
⅓ cup seasoned breadcrumbs
1 teaspoon seasoned salt
1 (14 ounce) can artichokes, drained, chopped
1 (10 ounce) can cream of celery soup
¾ cup shredded parmesan cheese

▣ Squeeze spinach between paper towels to
completely remove excess moisture.

▣ Combine spinach, onion, bell pepper, butter,
cheese, breadcrumbs, seasoned salt and
artichokes in sprayed slow cooker.

▣ Heat soup and ¼ cup water in saucepan to thin
and pour over vegetables. Cover and cook on
LOW for 5 to 7 hours.

▣ Sprinkle with parmesan cheese just before
serving. Serves 8 to 10.

Zucchini-Squash Combo

1½ pounds small yellow squash, peeled, cubed
1½ pounds zucchini, peeled, cubed
1 teaspoon seasoned salt
¼ cup (½ stick) butter, melted
½ cup seasoned breadcrumbs
½ cup shredded cheddar cheese

■ Place squash in sprayed slow cooker and sprinkle with seasoned salt and pepper.

■ Pour melted butter over squash and sprinkle with breadcrumbs and cheese. Cover and cook on LOW for 5 to 6 hours. Serves 6 to 8.

Slow cookers meld flavors deliciously, but colors can fade over long cooking times, therefore you can "dress up" your dish with colorful garnishes such as fresh parsley or chives, salsas, extra shredded cheeses, and a sprinkle of paprika or a dollop of sour cream.

Garden Casserole

1 pound yellow squash, sliced
1 pound zucchini, sliced
1 green bell pepper, seeded, chopped
1 red bell pepper, seeded, chopped
3 ribs celery, sliced
2 (10 ounce) cans cream of chicken soup
½ cup (1 stick) plus 3 tablespoons butter
1 (6 ounce) box herb stuffing mix

- Combine squash, zucchini, bell peppers and celery in large bowl; gently stir until soup mixes with vegetables.

- Melt ½ cup butter in skillet and add stuffing mix; mix well and set aside 1 cup for topping. Stir into vegetable-soup mixture and spoon into sprayed slow cooker. Cover and cook on LOW for 3 to 5 hours.

- Reheat the stuffing in skillet and sprinkle over top of vegetables. Drizzle 3 tablespoons melted butter over top; serve immediately. Serves 8 to 10.

Italian-Style Beans and Rice

1 (16 ounce) package frozen chopped bell peppers
     and onions, thawed
2 (15 ounce) cans Italian stewed tomatoes
1 (4 ounce) can diced green chilies
2 (15 ounce) cans great northern beans,
     rinsed, drained
1 teaspoon Italian seasoning
1 (14 ounce) can chicken broth
¼ teaspoon cayenne pepper
2 cups instant rice

   Combine bell peppers and onions, stewed
   tomatoes, green chilies, beans, Italian
   seasoning, broth and ½ cup water in sprayed
   slow cooker. Cover and cook on LOW for
   5 to 7 hours.

   Stir in cayenne pepper and rice, cover and
   cook for 30 minutes or until rice is tender.
   Serves 8.

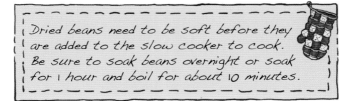

*Dried beans need to be soft before they
are added to the slow cooker to cook.
Be sure to soak beans overnight or soak
for 1 hour and boil for about 10 minutes.*

Big Bean Mix

2 (15 ounce) cans garbanzo beans, drained
1 (15 ounce) can red kidney beans, drained
1 (15 ounce) can cannellini beans, drained
2 (15 ounce) cans great northern beans, drained
1 teaspoon Italian seasoning
1 (1 ounce) packet onion soup mix
1 teaspoon minced garlic
½ cup beef broth

Combine all ingredients in sprayed slow
cooker and stir well. Cover and cook on
LOW for 5 to 6 hours or on HIGH for
2 hours 30 minutes to 3 hours. Serves 6 to 8.

Corn-Bean Mix-up

1 (15 ounce) can pinto beans, drained
1 (15 ounce) can black beans, rinsed, drained
1 (10 ounce) package frozen corn
1 (15 ounce) can tomato sauce
1 (1 ounce) packet chili seasoning
2 (15 ounce) cans Mexican stewed tomatoes
    with liquid

Combine pinto beans, black beans, corn,
tomato sauce, chili seasoning, tomatoes and
1 cup water in sprayed slow cooker; mix well.
Cover and cook on LOW for 6 to 7 hours.
Serves 6.

Bountiful Bean Bake

2 (15 ounce) cans navy beans, rinsed, drained
1 (15 ounce) can butter beans, rinsed, drained
1 (12 ounce) package grated carrots
1 (10 ounce) package frozen chopped bell peppers
    and onions, thawed
2 ribs celery, sliced
1 teaspoon dried marjoram
½ - 1 pound cooked smoked sausage, cut into
    ½-inch slices
½ cup chicken broth

 Combine beans, carrots, bell peppers and
onions, celery, marjoram, sausage, broth and
½ teaspoon salt in sprayed slow cooker.

Cover and cook on LOW for 6 to 8 hours. Stir
before serving. Serves 6.

TIP: Serve with cornbread and a salad to make a meal.

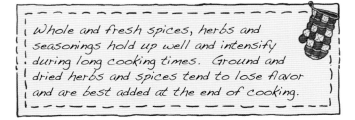

Whole and fresh spices, herbs and
seasonings hold up well and intensify
during long cooking times. Ground and
dried herbs and spices tend to lose flavor
and are best added at the end of cooking.

Creamy Rice Casserole

2 (6 ounce) boxes long grain-wild rice mix
1 (10 ounce) can cream of chicken soup
½ cup (1 stick) butter, melted
1 (10 ounce) package frozen chopped bell peppers
    and onions, thawed
3 ribs celery, thinly sliced
1 (4 ounce) can diced pimentos
1 (8 ounce) package shredded Velveeta® cheese

- Place rice mix, contents of seasoning packet,
  butter, bell peppers and onions, celery,
  pimentos and cheese in sprayed slow cooker.

- Heat soup and 2½ cups water in saucepan and
  stir to thin. Pour over rice and stir.

- Cover and cook on LOW for 6 to 10 hours
  or on HIGH for 2 to 3 hours 30 minutes.
  Serves 6 to 8.

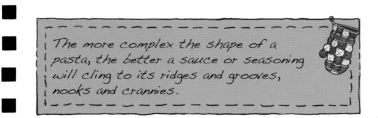

The more complex the shape of a pasta, the better a sauce or seasoning will cling to its ridges and grooves, nooks and crannies.

Autumn Rice Bake

1 cup brown rice
1½ cups orange juice
1 apple, peeled, cored, chopped
⅓ cup Craisins®
⅓ cup chopped pecans
2 tablespoons brown sugar
½ teaspoon ground cinnamon

Place rice, orange juice, apple, Craisins®,
pecans, brown sugar, cinnamon and
½ teaspoon salt in sprayed slow cooker. Cover
and cook on LOW for 4 to 5 hours. Serves 4.

Carnival Couscous

1 (5.7 ounce) box herbed-chicken couscous
1 red bell pepper, seeded, julienned
1 green bell pepper, seeded, julienned
2 small yellow squash, sliced
1 (16 ounce) package frozen mixed vegetables, thawed
1 (10 ounce) can French onion soup
¼ cup (½ stick) butter, melted
½ teaspoon seasoned salt

Combine all ingredients with 1½ cups water in
sprayed slow cooker and mix well. Cover and
cook on LOW for 2 to 4 hours. Serves 4.

Creamy Spinach Noodles

1 (12 ounce) package medium noodles
1 cup half-and-half cream
1 (10 ounce) package frozen chopped spinach,
    thawed
6 tablespoons (¾ stick) butter, melted
2 teaspoons seasoned salt
1½ cups shredded cheddar–Monterey Jack cheese

 Cook noodles according to package directions
    and drain. Place in sprayed slow cooker. Add
    half-and-half cream, spinach, butter and
    seasoned salt and stir until they blend well.
    Cover and cook on LOW for 2 to 3 hours.

 When ready to serve, fold in cheese. Serves 4.

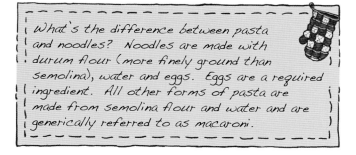

What's the difference between pasta
and noodles? Noodles are made with
durum flour (more finely ground than
semolina), water and eggs. Eggs are a required
ingredient. All other forms of pasta are
made from semolina flour and water and are
generically referred to as macaroni.

Yummy Bread Stuffing

¾ cup (1½ sticks) butter
2 medium onions, finely chopped
3 ribs celery, sliced
12 cups day-old bread cubes
2 teaspoons dried sage
1 teaspoon poultry seasoning
1 (32 ounce) carton chicken broth
2 eggs, beaten

 Melt butter in skillet and cook onion and celery until they are translucent, about 10 minutes. Place in large bowl and add bread cubes, sage and poultry seasoning.

Stir in just enough broth to moisten. (You may not use all the broth.) Stir in beaten eggs and spoon into sprayed slow cooker.

Cover and cook on HIGH for 45 minutes; reduce heat to LOW and cook for 4 to 6 hours. Serves 12.

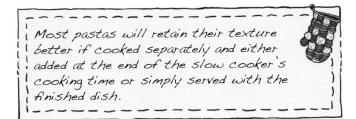

Most pastas will retain their texture better if cooked separately and either added at the end of the slow cooker's cooking time or simply served with the finished dish.

Main Dishes

Beef, Chicken, Pork and Seafood

Cheeseburger Pie Supper

1 (5 ounce) box bacon and cheddar scalloped
    potatoes
⅓ cup milk
¼ cup (½ stick) butter, melted
1½ pounds lean ground beef
1 onion, coarsely chopped
Canola oil
1 (15 ounce) can whole kernel corn with liquid
1 (8 ounce) package shredded cheddar cheese

 Place scalloped potatoes in sprayed slow
    cooker. Pour 2¼ cups boiling water, milk
    and butter over potatoes.

 Brown ground beef and onion in little oil
    in skillet, drain and spoon over potatoes.
    Top with corn. Cover and cook on LOW for
    6 to 7 hours.

 When ready to serve, sprinkle cheese over top.
    Serves 4 to 6.

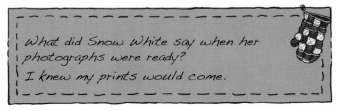

What did Snow White say when her
photographs were ready?
I knew my prints would come.

Pop's Beef-Potato Supper

2 pounds lean ground beef
1 (10 ounce) package frozen, chopped bell peppers
    and onions, thawed
3 ribs celery, sliced
1 (18 ounce) package frozen tater tots, thawed
1 (8 ounce) package shredded Velveeta® cheese
2 (10 ounce) cans cream of mushroom soup
1 soup can milk
1 (8 ounce) package shredded cheddar cheese

Cook ground beef in skillet over medium-high
heat about 10 minutes or until beef is no
longer pink; stir often. Drain and place in
sprayed slow cooker.

Combine bell peppers and onions, celery,
tater tots and Velveeta® cheese in bowl. Heat
soup and milk in saucepan just enough to thin
soup. Pour over vegetables and stir well.

Cover and cook on LOW for 6 to 8 hours.
Sprinkle with cheese. Serves 8 to 10.

"Waiter! This coffee tastes like dirt."
"Yes, sir. It's fresh ground."

Colorful Stuffed Peppers

6 medium red or green bell peppers, stemmed,
    seeded
1 pound lean ground beef
½ cup finely chopped onion
¾ cup instant rice
1 (15 ounce) can black beans, rinsed, drained
⅓ cup seasoned breadcrumbs
1 (8 ounce) package shredded Monterey Jack
    cheese, divided
1 (16 ounce) jar hot chunky salsa, divided

◻ Cook and brown ground beef in large skillet
   and stir to crumble. Drain, stir in onion, rice,
   beans, breadcrumbs, half cheese and half salsa
   and mix well. Spoon filling into bell peppers
   and place tops on each.

◻ Place ¾ cup water and remaining salsa in
   sprayed slow cooker. Arrange stuffed peppers
   around sides of cooker.

◻ Cover and cook on LOW for 6 to 7 hours or on
   HIGH for 3 hours to 3 hours 30 minutes.

◻ Transfer stuffed peppers to serving plate and
   sprinkle remaining cheese over tops. Serves 6.

*TIP: These peppers can be served over hot cooked rice with
      sauce from slow cooker poured over the rice.*

Meat Loaf Magic

1½ pounds lean ground beef
⅔ cup cracker crumbs
2 eggs, beaten
2 tablespoons plus ½ cup ketchup, divided
¼ cup finely minced onion
¼ cup packed brown sugar
1 teaspoon mustard
½ teaspoon ground nutmeg

■ Make foil handles for meat loaf by cutting
  3 (3 x 18-inch) strips of heavy foil. Place in
  bottom of slow cooker in crisscross strips and
  fold ends over top.

■ Combine beef, cracker crumbs, eggs,
  2 tablespoons ketchup, onion, and about
  1 teaspoon each of salt and pepper in large
  bowl. Shape into loaf and place in sprayed
  slow cooker. Fold ends of foil strips over loaf.
  Cover and cook on LOW for 5 to 6 hours.

■ A few minutes before serving, combine
  remaining ketchup, brown sugar, mustard and
  nutmeg in bowl and spoon over meatloaf. Cover
  and cook on HIGH for about 15 additional
  minutes. Lift meat loaf out with foil handles.
  Serves 6.

Italian Tortellini

½ pound ground round steak
1 (1 pound) package bulk Italian sausage
1 (15 ounce) carton refrigerated marinara sauce
1 (15 ounce) can Italian stewed tomatoes with liquid
1½ cups sliced fresh mushrooms
1 (9 ounce) package refrigerated cheese tortellini
1½ cups shredded mozzarella cheese

■ Brown and cook ground beef and sausage in
large skillet for about 10 minutes on medium-
low heat and drain.

■ Combine meat mixture, marinara sauce,
tomatoes and mushrooms in sprayed slow
cooker. Cover and cook on LOW 6 to
8 hours.

■ Stir in tortellini and sprinkle with mozzarella
cheese. Turn cooker to HIGH, cover and
cook for additional 10 to 15 minutes or until
tortellini is tender. Serves 4 to 6.

Two cannibals are eating a clown. one
says to the other, "Does this taste
funny to you?"

Green Chile-Beef Bake

1½ pounds lean ground beef
1 (10 ounce) package frozen chopped bell peppers
    and onions, thawed
1 (1 ounce) packet taco seasoning mix
2 (7 ounce) cans whole green chilies
1 (15 ounce) can refried beans
1 (16 ounce) jar thick-and-chunky salsa
8 - 10 cups slightly crushed tortilla chips
1 (12 ounce) package shredded Mexican
    4-cheese blend

   Brown beef in skillet and drain. Add bell
   peppers and onions and cook over medium
   heat for about 10 minutes. Stir in taco
   seasoning and ¼ cup water.

   Cut chilies in half, remove seeds and arrange
   evenly in sprayed slow cooker. Add beef
   mixture and add refried beans evenly over
   beef. Top with remaining chilies. Pour salsa
   over all top. Do not stir. Cover and cook on
   LOW for 8 to 10 hours.

   Place about ¾ cup crushed tortilla chips
   on individual plates, spoon beef mixture
   over chips and top with about ¼ cup cheese.
   Serves 8 to 10.

Slow Cooker Ziti

1 pound ground beef
1 tablespoon Italian seasoning
2 (26 ounce) cans spaghetti sauce
2 (8 ounce) packages shredded mozzarella
    cheese, divided
1 (15 ounce) carton ricotta cheese
1 cup grated parmesan cheese
1 (16 ounce) box ziti noodles

■ Brown ground beef in skillet and drain. Add Italian seasoning, sauce and 1 teaspoon each salt and pepper to meat.

■ Combine 1 package mozzarella, ricotta and parmesan in separate bowl.

■ In slow cooker, layer 2 cups meat mixture, half ziti and half cheese mixture. Repeat. Cover with remaining meat mixture. Cover and cook on LOW for 5 to 6 hours.

■ Top with remaining mozzarella and serve when cheese melts. Serves 6 to 8.

Crowd-Pleasing Pepper Steak

¼ cup flour
1½ pounds beef round steak
2 tablespoons canola oil
1 onion, chopped
2 large green bell peppers, seeded,
        julienned, divided
1 (15 ounce) can Italian stewed tomatoes
½ cup beef broth
1 tablespoon Worcestershire sauce
1 cup instant rice

▨ Combine flour, 1 teaspoon each of salt and
    pepper in shallow bowl. Cut steak into strips
    and toss with flour mixture to coat thoroughly.
    Heat oil in skillet and cook steak strips until
    slightly brown; turn often.

▨ Place steak, onion, 1 julienned bell pepper,
    tomatoes, broth and Worcestershire in sprayed
    slow cooker. Cover and cook on LOW for
    7 to 9 hours.

▨ Add remaining julienned pepper to slow
    cooker, cover and cook for 1 additional hour.

▨ Cook rice according to package directions,
    place on serving platter and top with pepper
    steak. Serves 4.

Spectacular Beef and Broccoli

1 - 1½ pounds boneless round steak, cut into
    1-inch cubes
1 (10 ounce) package frozen chopped bell peppers
    and onions, thawed
2 ribs celery, cut in 1-inch slices
1 (10 ounce) can beef broth
3 tablespoons teriyaki baste-and-glaze
2 tablespoons cornstarch
1 (16 ounce) package frozen broccoli florets, thawed
Rice, cooked

 Place steak cubes, bell peppers and onions,
celery, broth, teriyaki baste-and-glaze and
½ teaspoon pepper in sprayed slow cooker.
Cover and cook on LOW for 8 to 10 hours.

 Mix cornstarch with 2 to 3 tablespoons water
in small bowl. Stir cornstarch mixture and
broccoli florets into slow cooker, cover and
cook for additional 25 to 30 minutes. Serve
over rice. Serves 4 to 6.

*When purchasing ground beef, remember
that fat greatly contributes to its
flavor. The lower the fat content, the
drier it will be once cooked.*

Beef Roulades

1½ pounds beef flank steak
5 slices bacon
¾ cup finely chopped onion
1 (4 ounce) can mushrooms pieces
1 tablespoon Worcestershire sauce
⅓ cup Italian-seasoned breadcrumbs
1 (12 ounce) jar beef gravy
Mashed potatoes

Cut steak into 4 to 6 serving-size pieces. Cut bacon into small pieces and combine with onion, mushrooms, Worcestershire and breadcrumbs in bowl.

Place about ½ cup onion mixture on each piece of steak. Roll meat and secure ends with toothpicks. Dry beef rolls with paper towels. In skillet, brown steak rolls and transfer to sprayed slow cooker.

Pour gravy evenly over steaks to thoroughly moisten. Cover and cook on LOW for 7 to 9 hours. Serve with mashed potatoes. Serves 4 to 6.

TIP: This is really good served with mashed potatoes. Have you tried instant mashed potatoes as a time-saver?

Teriyaki Steak

1½ - 2 pounds flank steak
1 (15 ounce) can sliced pineapple with juice
1 tablespoon marinade for chicken
⅓ cup packed brown sugar
3 tablespoons soy sauce
½ teaspoon ground ginger
1 (14 ounce) can chicken broth
1 cup long grain rice

▨ Roll flank steak, tie in place and cut into
7 to 8 individual steaks.

▨ Combine ½ cup pineapple juice, marinade
for chicken, brown sugar, soy sauce and
ginger in bowl large enough for marinade
to cover individual steaks. Add steak rolls
and marinate for 1 hour in sauce. Discard
marinade.

▨ Pour chicken broth into sprayed slow cooker.
Add rice and ¾ cup water. Place steaks over
rice and broth. Cover and cook on LOW for
8 to 10 hours. Serves 4 to 6.

Round Steak Stroganoff

2 pounds beef round steak
¾ cup flour, divided
½ teaspoon mustard
2 onions, thinly sliced
½ pound fresh mushrooms, sliced
1 (10 ounce) can beef broth
¼ cup dry white wine or cooking wine
1 (8 ounce) carton sour cream
Rice or noodles, cooked

■ Trim excess fat from steak and cut into 3-inch strips about ½-inch wide.

■ Combine ½ cup flour, mustard and a little salt and pepper in bowl and toss with steak strips. Place strips in sprayed, oval slow cooker.

■ Cover with onions and mushrooms. Add beef broth and wine. Cover and cook on LOW for 8 to 10 hours.

■ Just before serving, combine sour cream and ¼ cup flour in bowl. Stir into cooker and cook for additional 10 to 15 minutes or until stroganoff thickens slightly. Serve over cooked rice or noodles. Serves 4 to 6.

Mushroom Round Steak

1½ - 2 pounds round steak
1 (1 ounce) packet onion soup mix
½ cup dry red wine
1 (8 ounce) carton fresh mushrooms, sliced
1 (10 ounce) can French onion soup

▨ Cut round steak in serving-size pieces and place in sprayed oval slow cooker.

▨ Combine soup mix, red wine, mushrooms, French onion soup and ½ cup water in bowl. Spoon over steak pieces.

▨ Cover and cook on LOW for 7 to 8 hours. Serves 4 to 6.

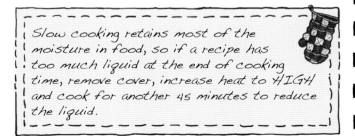

Slow cooking retains most of the moisture in food, so if a recipe has too much liquid at the end of cooking time, remove cover, increase heat to HIGH and cook for another 45 minutes to reduce the liquid.

Pasta with Seasoned Beef Tips

2 - 2½ pounds lean beef stew meat
2 cups frozen, small whole onions, thawed
1 green bell pepper, seeded
1 (6 ounce) jar pitted Greek olives or ripe olives
½ cup sun-dried tomatoes in oil, drained, chopped
1 (28 ounce) jar marinara sauce
1 (8 ounce) package pasta twirls, cooked

 Place beef and onions in sprayed slow cooker. Cut bell pepper in 1-inch cubes and add to slow cooker.

 Add olives and tomatoes and pour marinara sauce over top. Cover and cook on LOW for 8 to 10 hours. Serve over pasta twirls. Serves 4 to 6.

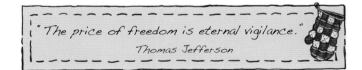

"The price of freedom is eternal vigilance."
Thomas Jefferson

Favorite Pot Roast and Veggies

1 (2 pound) chuck roast
4 - 5 medium potatoes, peeled, quartered
4 large carrots, quartered
1 onion, quartered
1 (14 ounce) can beef broth, divided
2 tablespoons cornstarch

■ Trim fat from pieces of roast. Cut roast into
2 equal pieces. Brown pieces of roast in skillet.
(Coat pieces with flour, salt and pepper if you'd
like a little "breading" on the outside.)

■ Place potatoes, carrots and onion in sprayed
slow cooker and mix well. Place browned beef
over vegetables. Pour 1½ cups broth over beef
and vegetables. Set aside remaining broth and
refrigerate.

■ Cover and cook on LOW for 8 to 9 hours.
About 5 minutes before serving, remove beef
and vegetables with slotted spoon and place on
serving platter. Cover to keep warm.

■ Pour liquid from slow cooker into medium
saucepan. Blend remaining ½ cup broth and
cornstarch in bowl until smooth and add to
liquid in saucepan. Boil for 1 minute and stir
constantly to thicken for gravy.

■ Serve gravy with roast and veggies; season with a
little salt and pepper, if desired. Serves 4 to 6.

Herb-Crusted Beef Roast

1 (2 - 3 pound) beef rump roast
¼ cup chopped fresh parsley
¼ cup chopped fresh oregano leaves
½ teaspoon dried rosemary leaves
1 teaspoon minced garlic
1 tablespoon oil
6 slices thick-cut bacon

■ Rub roast with a little salt and pepper.
  Combine parsley, oregano, rosemary, garlic
  and oil in small bowl and press mixture on
  top and sides of roast.

■ Place roast in sprayed slow cooker. Place
  bacon over top of beef and tuck ends under.
  Cover and cook on LOW for 6 to 8 hours.
  Serves 4 to 6.

Slow cookers aren't just for cooking
when it's cold and wintry outside. It's
also great to use in the summer so you
don't heat up the kitchen from the oven and
you use much less energy with the slow
cooker than the oven.

Smoked Brisket

1 (4 - 6 pound) trimmed brisket
1 (4 ounce) bottle liquid smoke
Garlic salt
Celery salt
Worcestershire sauce
1 onion, chopped
1 (6 ounce) bottle barbecue sauce

Place brisket in large shallow dish and pour liquid smoke over top. Sprinkle with garlic salt and celery salt. Cover and refrigerate overnight.

Before cooking, drain liquid smoke and douse brisket with Worcestershire sauce. Place chopped onion in slow cooker and place brisket on top of onion. Cover and cook on LOW for 6 to 8 hours.

Pour barbecue sauce over brisket and cook for additional 1 hour. Serves 6 to 8.

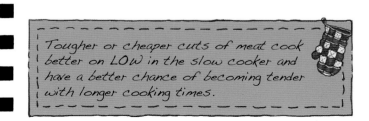

Tougher or cheaper cuts of meat cook better on LOW in the slow cooker and have a better chance of becoming tender with longer cooking times.

Sweet and Spicy Brisket

½ cup packed brown sugar
1 tablespoon Cajun seasoning
2 teaspoons lemon pepper
1 tablespoon Worcestershire sauce
1 (3 - 4 pound) trimmed beef brisket

- Combine brown sugar, Cajun seasoning, lemon pepper and Worcestershire in small bowl and spread over brisket.

- Place brisket in sprayed oval slow cooker. Cover and cook on LOW for 6 to 8 hours. Serves 6 to 8.

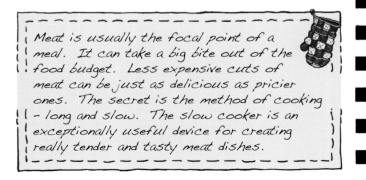

Meat is usually the focal point of a meal. It can take a big bite out of the food budget. Less expensive cuts of meat can be just as delicious as pricier ones. The secret is the method of cooking - long and slow. The slow cooker is an exceptionally useful device for creating really tender and tasty meat dishes.

Corned Beef Supper

2 - 3 pounds corned eye of round beef
9 peppercorns
¼ cup red wine vinegar
1 (12 ounce) package baby carrots
6 medium potatoes, peeled, halved
1 medium head cabbage, coarsely sliced in 6 wedges

Place beef, peppercorns, vinegar and 7 cups water in sprayed slow cooker. Arrange carrots and potatoes around beef. Cover and cook on LOW for 8 to 10 hours.

Place cabbage wedges around sides of slow cooker and cook for additional 15 to 20 minutes. Discard liquid in slow cooker. Serves 6.

TIP: In order to keep cabbage pieces together during cooking, leave a bit of the core with each wedge.

"Doc, I can't stop singing 'The Green, Green Grass of Home."

"That sounds like Tom Jones Syndrome."

"Is it common?"

"Well, it's not unusual."

Justice with Short Ribs

Flour for coating ribs
3 pounds beef short ribs
3 tablespoons olive oil
1 onion, thinly sliced
½ cup chili sauce
¼ cup packed brown sugar
3 tablespoons vinegar
2 tablespoons flour

■ Coat ribs with lots of salt and pepper; then dredge in flour, coating well. Brown short ribs in oil in large skillet on medium-high heat until light brown.

■ Place onion, chili sauce, brown sugar and vinegar in sprayed slow cooker; mix thoroughly. Add browned ribs. Cover and cook on LOW for 6 to 8 hours.

■ Remove ribs to serving platter and turn slow cooker to HIGH heat. Combine 2 tablespoons flour with ½ cup water in bowl and stir into sauce in slow cooker. Cook for 10 minutes or until mixture thickens. Spoon sauce over ribs. Serves 6.

Back Yard Supper

1 (8 count) package beef wieners
1 onion, finely chopped
2 (15 ounce) can chili with beans
1 (10 ounce) can diced tomatoes and green chilies
1 teaspoon ground cumin
1 (8 ounce) package shredded Velveeta® cheese
Hot dog buns

■ Combine wieners, onion, chili, tomatoes
   and green chilies, and cumin in sprayed slow
   cooker. Cover and cook on LOW for 5 to
   7 hours or on HIGH for 2 hours 30 minutes.

■ Stir in cheese just before serving and allow
   cheese to melt. Serve each wiener on hot dog
   bun and spoon sauce over top. Serves 8.

TIP: Sprinkle a little extra cheese on top.

Southwestern Chicken Pot

6 boneless, skinless chicken breast halves
1 teaspoon ground cumin
1 teaspoon chili powder
1 (10 ounce) can cream of chicken soup
1 (10 ounce) can fiesta nacho cheese soup
1 cup salsa
Rice or noodles, cooked
Flour tortillas

Sprinkle chicken breasts with cumin, chili powder, and a little salt and pepper and place in sprayed oval slow cooker.

Combine soups and salsa in saucepan. Heat just enough to mix well and pour over chicken breasts. Cover and cook on LOW for 6 to 7 hours. Serve over rice or noodles with warmed flour tortillas spread with butter. Serves 4 to 6.

Some flavors, such as chili powder and garlic, will become more intense during cooking. Others tend to "cook out" and lose their flavor. It is always wise to taste at the end of cooking and season as needed.

Hot Shot Chicken

4 boneless, skinless chicken breast halves
4 green onions with tops, chopped
I teaspoon dried rosemary
I teaspoon dried sage
I teaspoon dried thyme
3 cloves garlic, minced
I (12 ounce) bottle or can beer

Preheat broiler.

Sprinkle salt and pepper generously over
chicken. Place in sprayed baking dish and
broil in oven to brown chicken on both sides.

Place chicken in sprayed slow cooker and
sprinkle with onions, rosemary, sage, thyme
and garlic. Pour beer around chicken and
cook on LOW for 4 hours. Serves 4.

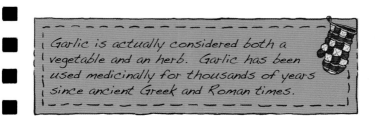

Garlic is actually considered both a
vegetable and an herb. Garlic has been
used medicinally for thousands of years
since ancient Greek and Roman times.

Picante Chicken

4 boneless, skinless chicken breast halves
1 green bell pepper, seeded, cut in rings
1 (16 ounce) jar picante sauce
⅓ cup packed brown sugar
1 tablespoon mustard

- Place chicken breasts in sprayed slow cooker with bell pepper rings over top of chicken.

- Combine picante, brown sugar and mustard in bowl and spoon over top of chicken. Cover and cook on LOW for 4 to 5 hours. Serves 4.

Chicken Fajitas

2 pounds boneless, skinless chicken breast halves
1 onion, thinly sliced
1 red bell pepper, seeded, julienned
1 teaspoon ground cumin
1½ teaspoons chili powder
1 tablespoon lime juice
½ cup chicken broth
8 - 10 warm flour tortillas
Guacamole
Sour cream
Lettuce and tomatoes

■ Cut chicken into diagonal strips and place
in sprayed slow cooker. Top with onion and
bell pepper.

■ Combine cumin, chili powder, lime juice and
chicken broth in bowl and pour over chicken
and vegetables. Cover and cook on LOW for
5 to 7 hours.

■ Serve several slices of chicken mixture
with sauce into center of each warm tortilla
and fold. Serve with guacamole, sour
cream, lettuce and/or tomatoes or plain.
Serves 4 to 6.

Pizza-Parmesan Chicken

1 large egg, beaten
1 cup seasoned breadcrumbs
2 tablespoons canola oil
6 boneless, skinless chicken breast halves
1 (10 ounce) jar pizza sauce
⅔ cup grated parmesan cheese
6 slices mozzarella cheese

▢ Place egg in shallow bowl. In separate shallow
bowl, place breadcrumbs. Dip chicken breasts
into egg and then into breadcrumbs. Press
crumbs on all sides of chicken. Heat oil in
large skillet and saute chicken.

▢ Arrange one layer of chicken in sprayed slow
cooker and pour half pizza sauce on top. Add
second layer of chicken and pour remaining
sauce over top. Cover and cook on LOW for
6 to 8 hours or just until chicken is tender but
not dry.

▢ Sprinkle with parmesan cheese and add
mozzarella slices on top; cover and cook for
additional 15 minutes. Serves 6.

Rolled Chicken Florentine

6 boneless, skinless chicken breast halves
6 thin slices ham
6 slices Swiss cheese
1 (10 ounce) package frozen chopped spinach,
    thawed, well drained*
1 (16 ounce) package baby carrots
2 (10 ounce) cans cream of chicken soup
1 (10 ounce) box chicken-flavored rice

▨ With flat side of meat mallet, pound chicken
to ¼-inch thickness. Place ham slice, cheese
slice and ¼ cup spinach on each chicken piece
and roll chicken from short end, jellyroll-
style. Secure each roll with toothpick.

▨ Place carrots in sprayed slow cooker and
top with chicken rolls. Heat soup with a
little water in saucepan just to thin and
pour over rolls. Cover and cook on LOW
for 6 to 8 hours.

▨ Cook rice according to package directions and
serve carrots, chicken rolls and sauce over rice.
Serves 6.

*TIP: *Squeeze spinach between paper towels to completely
    remove excess moisture.*

Colorful Chicken with Cashews

5 boneless, skinless chicken breast halves, cut into
        1-inch strips
2 ribs celery, sliced
¼ cup soy sauce
¼ teaspoon ginger
½ cup chicken broth
1 (8 ounce) can sliced bamboo shoots, drained
½ cup Chinese pea pods
½ cup cashews, toasted
2 tablespoons cornstarch
Rice, cooked

■ Place chicken strips and celery in sprayed slow
   cooker. Add soy sauce, ginger, broth and a
   little salt and pepper.

■ Cover and cook on LOW for 4 to 4 hours
   30 minutes.

■ Increase heat to HIGH and add bamboo
   shoots, pea pods and cashews. Dissolve
   cornstarch in 2 tablespoons water in bowl and
   stir into slow cooker.

■ Cover and cook for about 25 minutes or until
   thickened, stirring once. Serve over rice.
   Serves 6.

Never-Fail Chicken Spaghetti

6 boneless, skinless chicken breast halves,
    cooked, cubed
2 (10 ounce) cans cream of chicken soup
½ cup milk
1 (4 ounce) can sliced mushrooms, drained
¼ cup (½ stick) butter, melted
1 (12 ounce) package thin spaghetti
1 (5 ounce) package grated parmesan cheese

■ Combine chicken, mushrooms and butter in
   sprayed slow cooker; stir until blended well.
   Cover and cook on LOW for 6 to 8 hours.

■ Cook spaghetti according to package
   instructions and place on serving platter.
   Spoon chicken mixture and sauce over
   spaghetti and top with cheese. Serves 6 to 8.

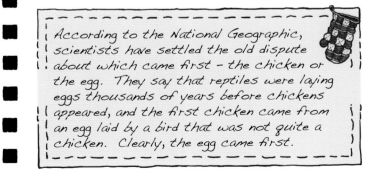

*According to the National Geographic,
scientists have settled the old dispute
about which came first – the chicken or
the egg. They say that reptiles were laying
eggs thousands of years before chickens
appeared, and the first chicken came from
an egg laid by a bird that was not quite a
chicken. Clearly, the egg came first.*

Stuff-it Chicken

5 boneless, skinless chicken breast halves
2 (10 ounce) cans cream of chicken soup
1 (6 ounce) box chicken stuffing mix
1 (16 ounce) package frozen green peas, thawed

■ Place chicken breasts in sprayed large slow
   cooker. Heat cream of chicken soup with
   a little water in a saucepan to thin. Pour
   over chicken.

■ Combine stuffing mix with ingredients on
   package directions in bowl and spoon over
   chicken and soup. Cover and cook on LOW
   for 5 to 6 hours.

■ Sprinkle drained green peas over top of
   stuffing. Cover and cook for additional
   45 to 50 minutes. Serves 4 to 5.

*TIP: For a nice variation, substitute 1 (10 ounce) can fiesta
      nacho cheese soup for 1 can of cream of chicken soup.*

Mushroom Chicken

4 boneless, skinless chicken breasts halves
1 (15 ounce) can tomato sauce
2 (4 ounce) cans sliced mushrooms, drained
1 (10 ounce) package frozen chopped bell peppers
    and onions
2 teaspoons Italian seasoning
1 teaspoon minced garlic

Brown chicken breasts in skillet and place in
sprayed oval slow cooker.

Combine tomato sauce, mushrooms, onions
and peppers, Italian seasoning, garlic, and
¼ cup water in bowl and spoon over chicken
breasts. Cover and cook on LOW for 4 to
5 hours. Serves 4.

Chicken a la Orange

5 - 6 boneless, skinless chicken breast halves
1 - 2 tablespoons salt-free garlic and herb seasoning
2 (11 ounce) cans mandarin oranges, drained
1 (6 ounce) can frozen orange juice concentrate
1 tablespoon lemon juice
1 (10 ounce) can chicken broth
2 tablespoons cornstarch
2 - 3 cups cooked rice

▪ Place chicken breasts in sprayed slow cooker
and sprinkle with garlic-herb seasoning.

▪ Combine oranges, orange juice concentrate,
lemon juice, broth, cornstarch and ⅓ cup
water in bowl, mix well. Pour mixture into
slow cooker. Cover and cook on LOW for
6 to 8 hours.

▪ Place cooked rice on serving platter and top
with chicken and sauce. Serves 5 to 6.

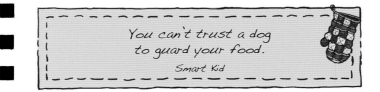

*You can't trust a dog
to guard your food.*

Smart Kid

Oregano Chicken

½ cup (1 stick) butter, melted
1 (1 ounce) packet Italian salad dressing
1 tablespoon lemon juice
4 - 5 boneless, skinless chicken breast halves
2 tablespoons dried oregano

 Combine butter, dressing and lemon juice in
bowl and mix well.

Place chicken breasts in sprayed large slow
cooker. Spoon butter-lemon juice mixture
over chicken. Cover and cook on LOW for
4 to 5 hours.

Baste chicken with pan juices, sprinkle
oregano over chicken and cook 1 additional
hour. Serves 4 to 6.

TIP: *This recipe works well with boneless pork chops instead
of chicken. For a complete meal, add a 10 ounce can
French onion soup and serve over thin spaghetti.*

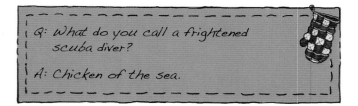

Q: What do you call a frightened
scuba diver?

A: Chicken of the sea.

Chicken and Artichokes

¼ cup (½ stick) plus 2 tablespoons butter, divided
6 boneless, skinless chicken breast halves
1 (14 ounce) jar water-packed artichoke
    hearts, drained
1 (8 ounce) can sliced water chestnuts, drained
2 red bell peppers, seeded, cut into strips
1 (14 ounce) can chicken broth
1 (10 ounce) can cream of celery soup
1 (8 ounce) package shredded Italian cheese
1½ cups seasoned breadcrumbs

Melt ¼ cup butter in large skillet on medium heat, lightly brown chicken and place in sprayed slow cooker.

Cut each artichoke heart in half and place artichokes, water chestnuts and bell peppers around chicken.

Combine broth, celery soup and cheese in bowl, mix well and pour over chicken-artichoke mixture. Cover and cook on LOW for 7 to 9 hours.

Ten minutes before serving, place breadcrumbs and 2 tablespoons melted butter in pan and stir until crumbs are well coated with butter. Heat in 325° oven for about 10 minutes. Sprinkle over dish. Serves 6.

Chicken and Pasta

1 onion, chopped
1 cup fresh mushroom halves
3 boneless, skinless chicken breast halves
1 (15 ounce) can Italian stewed tomatoes
1 teaspoon chicken bouillon granules
1 teaspoon minced garlic
1 teaspoon Italian seasoning
1 (8 ounce) package fettuccini
1 (4 ounce) package grated parmesan cheese

■ Place onion and mushrooms in sprayed slow
   cooker. Cut chicken into 1-inch pieces and
   place over vegetables.

■ Combine stewed tomatoes, chicken bouillon,
   garlic and Italian seasoning in small bowl.
   Pour over chicken. Cover and cook on LOW
   for 5 to 6 hours.

■ Cook fettuccini according to package
   directions and drain. Serve chicken over
   fettuccini and sprinkle with parmesan cheese.
   Serves 4.

TIP: Add ¼ cup butter for a richer taste.

Broccoli-Cheese Chicken

4 boneless, skinless chicken breast halves
2 tablespoons butter, melted
1 (10 ounce) can broccoli-cheese soup
¼ cup milk
1 (10 ounce) package frozen broccoli spears
Rice, cooked

■ Dry chicken breasts with paper towels and
   place in sprayed oval slow cooker.

■ Combine melted butter, soup and milk in bowl
   and spoon over chicken. Cover and cook on
   LOW for 4 to 6 hours.

■ Place broccoli over chicken. Cover and
   cook for additional 1 hour. Serve over rice.
   Serves 4.

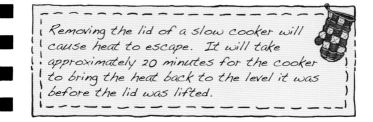

Removing the lid of a slow cooker will cause heat to escape. It will take approximately 20 minutes for the cooker to bring the heat back to the level it was before the lid was lifted.

Company Chicken Roll-Ups

6 boneless, skinless chicken breast halves
6 slices prosciutto
6 slices Mozzarella cheese
½ teaspoon dried sage
¾ cup chicken broth
2 ribs celery, thinly sliced
1 green bell pepper, seeded, chopped
3 tablespoons cornstarch
½ cup half-and-half cream
Rice, cooked

Place chicken between 2 sheets of wax paper
and pound with meat mallet to ½-inch thick.

Place each slice of prosciutto on wax paper,
top with chicken breast and slice of cheese.
Sprinkle with sage and a little salt and
pepper; roll jellyroll-style and secure with
toothpicks. Place in sprayed slow cooker.
Add chicken broth; cover and cook on LOW
for 5 to 6 hours.

Add celery and bell pepper. Dissolve
cornstarch in half-and-half cream in bowl and
stir into slow cooker. Increase heat to HIGH
and cook for additional 20 minutes or until
mixture has thickened. Serve over rice and
top roll-ups with sauce. Serves 6.

Everybody's Favorite Dumplings

4 large boneless, skinless chicken breast halves
¼ cup (½ stick) butter, melted
2 (10 ounce) cans cream of chicken soup
1 small onion, finely chopped
2 ribs celery, sliced
2 (10 ounce) packages refrigerated biscuits

▦ Place chicken breasts, butter, soup, onion and
celery in sprayed large slow cooker. Fill with
enough water to cover. Cover and cook on
HIGH for 5 to 6 hours.

▦ About 30 minutes before serving, remove
chicken breasts with slotted spoon and cut
chicken into small pieces, return to slow
cooker. Tear each biscuit into several pieces
and gradually drop pieces into slow cooker.
Cook until dough is no longer raw in center.

▦ Remove liner bowl from slow cooker and serve
right from the bowl. Serves 8.

Supreme Sun-Dried Chicken

3 pounds boneless, skinless chicken breast halves
1 tablespoon canola oil
1 teaspoon minced garlic
½ cup white wine (can use cooking wine)
1 (14 ounce) can chicken broth
1 teaspoon dried basil
¾ cup chopped sun-dried tomatoes
1 (10 ounce) box couscous

■ Cut chicken into 8 to 9 serving pieces. Heat oil in large skillet and brown several pieces at a time, making sure pieces brown evenly. Place each browned piece of chicken in sprayed large slow cooker.

■ Add garlic, wine, broth and basil to skillet and bring to a boil. Pour over chicken and scatter tomatoes on top. Cover and cook on LOW for 4 to 6 hours.

■ Cook couscous according to package directions and place on serving platter. Place chicken pieces on top of couscous. Serve sauce on the side. Serves 8.

Lemon-Herb Chicken Pasta

1 pound chicken tenders
Lemon-herb chicken seasoning
3 tablespoons butter
1 onion, coarsely chopped
1 (15 ounce) can diced tomatoes
1 (10 ounce) can golden mushroom soup
(8 ounce) box angel hair pasta

Pat chicken tenders dry with paper towels
and sprinkle with ample amount of chicken
seasoning. Melt butter in large skillet, brown
chicken and place in sprayed oval slow cooker.
Pour remaining butter and seasonings over
chicken and cover with onion.

Combine tomatoes and soup in bowl and pour
over chicken and onion. Cover and cook on
LOW for 4 to 5 hours.

Cook pasta according to package directions.
Serve chicken and sauce over pasta. Serves 4.

There are at least 350 different shapes
and sizes of pasta.

Easy Chicken Pie

1¼ pounds boneless, skinless chicken thighs
¼ cup finely chopped onion
1 (10 ounce) can chicken soup
1 cup milk, divided
2 ribs celery, thinly sliced
2¼ cups biscuit mix
1 (16 ounce) package frozen mixed vegetables, thawed

 Place chicken in sprayed slow cooker.

 Combine onion, soup, ⅓ cup milk and celery
in small bowl, mix well. Spoon over chicken.
Cover and cook on LOW for 8 to 10 hours.

 Prepare 8 biscuits using biscuit mix and
remaining milk as directed on package. While
biscuits are baking, gently stir vegetables into
chicken mixture. Increase heat to HIGH,
cover and cook for additional 15 minutes.

 To serve, split each biscuit and place bottoms
in individual soup bowls. Spoon about ¾ cup
chicken mixture on top of biscuits and place
tops of biscuits over chicken mixture. Serves 8.

Honey-Baked Chicken

2 small fryer chickens, quartered
½ cup (1 stick) butter, melted
⅔ cup honey
¼ cup dijon-style mustard
1 teaspoon curry powder

■ Place chicken pieces in sprayed large slow
cooker, breast-side up and sprinkle a little salt
over chicken.

■ Combine butter, honey, mustard and curry
powder in bowl and mix well. Pour over
chicken quarters. Cover and cook on LOW
for 6 to 8 hours. Baste chicken once during
cooking. Serves 6 to 8.

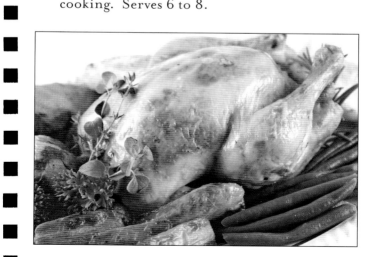

Monterey Bake

6 (6 inch) corn tortillas
3 cups cubed cooked chicken
1 (10 ounce) package frozen whole kernel corn
1 (15 ounce) can pinto beans with liquid
1 (16 ounce) jar hot salsa
¼ cup sour cream
1 tablespoon flour
3 tablespoons snipped fresh cilantro
1 (8 ounce) package shredded 4-cheese blend

 Preheat oven to 250°.

Cut tortillas into 6 wedges. Place half of tortillas wedges in sprayed slow cooker. Place remaining wedges on baking pan, bake for about 10 minutes and set aside.

Layer chicken, corn and beans over tortillas in cooker. Combine salsa, sour cream, flour and cilantro in bowl and pour over chicken, corn and beans. Cover and cook on LOW for 3 to 4 hours.

When ready to serve, place baked tortillas wedges and cheese on top of each serving. Serves 4 to 6.

Aloha Chicken

3 pounds boneless skinless chicken breast halves
1 (8 ounce) can crushed pineapple
1 tablespoon soy sauce
2 tablespoons mustard
1 cup packed brown sugar
½ cup (1 stick) butter, melted
½ cup lemon juice
½ cup honey

Place all ingredients in sprayed slow cooker.
Cover and cook on LOW for 4 to 5 hours, or
until chicken is thoroughly cooked. Serves 8.

A "free-range" chicken is one that is
given twice as much room as mass
produced chickens and they are free to
roam indoors and outdoors. This is
supposed to enhance the "chicken" flavor
because they are "happy" chickens.

Perfect Pork Chops and Potatoes

2 tablespoons canola oil
6 - 8 boneless pork chops
1 (10 ounce) can cream of chicken soup
1 tablespoon mustard
½ cup chicken broth
1 teaspoon minced garlic
6 - 8 red potatoes with peels, sliced
2 - 3 onions, sliced

■ Heat oil in skillet on medium-high heat and brown pork chops on both sides.

■ Combine soup, mustard, broth, garlic and a little salt and pepper in sprayed slow cooker. Layer potatoes and onions over mixture; place browned pork chops on top.

■ Cover and cook on LOW for 8 to 10 hours or on HIGH for 4 to 5 hours. Serves 6 to 8.

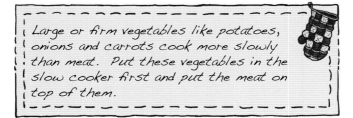

Large or firm vegetables like potatoes, onions and carrots cook more slowly than meat. Put these vegetables in the slow cooker first and put the meat on top of them.

Stuffed Pork Chops

4 - 5 (1-inch thick) pork chops
1 (15 ounce) can mixed vegetables, well drained
1 (8 ounce) can whole kernel corn, drained
½ cup rice
1 cup Italian-seasoned breadcrumbs
1 (15 ounce) can stewed tomatoes, slightly drained

 Cut pocket in each pork chop and season with a little salt and pepper. Combine vegetables, corn, rice and breadcrumbs in large bowl and stuff pork chops with mixture. Secure open sides with toothpicks.

Place remaining vegetable mixture in sprayed slow cooker. Add pork chops and spoon stewed tomatoes over top of pork chops. Cover and cook on LOW for 8 to 9 hours. Serves 4 to 5.

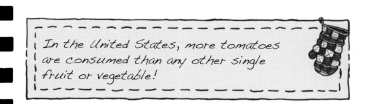

In the United States, more tomatoes are consumed than any other single fruit or vegetable!

Italian Pork Chops

6 - 8 (1-inch thick) boneless pork chops
½ pound fresh mushrooms, sliced
1 (10 ounce) package frozen chopped bell peppers
    and onions, thawed
1 teaspoon Italian seasoning
1 (15 ounce) can Italian stewed tomatoes

▧ Brown pork chops in skillet and sprinkle with
    salt and pepper on both sides.

▧ Combine mushrooms, bell peppers and
    onions, and Italian seasoning in sprayed large
    slow cooker. Place pork chops over vegetables
    and pour stewed tomatoes over pork chops.

▧ Cover and cook on LOW for 7 to 8 hours.
    Serves 6 to 8.

*Flavor is often enhanced by browning
meats before adding them to the slow
cooker. Meats can be dredged in seasoned
salt and flour or browned as is in a little oil.
The browning seals in the flavors and reduces
the fat to some extent. After browning,
deglaze the pan with a little liquid, stir all
the bits and pieces together and cook a little.
Add to slow cooker for more flavor.*

Pork Loin Topped with Pecans

½ cup finely ground pecans
1 teaspoon mustard
1 tablespoon brown sugar
1 (3 pound) pork loin
1 (14 ounce) can beef broth
2 tablespoons chili sauce
2 tablespoon lemon juice
1 (10 ounce) box plain couscous

■ Place ground pecans, mustard and brown
  sugar in small bowl and mix well. Press pecan
  mixture onto pork roast and place in sprayed
  slow cooker.

■ Combine broth, chili sauce and lemon juice
  in bowl and pour into slow cooker. Cover and
  cook on LOW for 8 to 10 hours.

■ Let stand for 10 minutes before slicing
  to serve.

■ Cook couscous according to package directions
  and place in serving bowl. Serve with sliced
  pork roast. Serves 8 to 10.

Our Best Pork Roast

1 (16 ounce) can whole cranberry sauce
½ cup quartered dried apricots
½ teaspoon grated orange peel
⅓ cup orange juice
1 large shallot, chopped
1 tablespoon cider vinegar
1 teaspoon mustard
2 tablespoons brown sugar
¼ teaspoon dried ginger
2 - 3 pound pork loin roast

■ Combine cranberry sauce, apricots, orange peel, orange juice, shallot, vinegar, mustard, brown sugar, ginger and 1 teaspoon salt in bowl. Stir mixture until well blended and spoon into sprayed slow cooker.

■ Trim roast of any fat and add roast to slow cooker. Spoon a little cranberry mixture on top. Cover and cook on LOW for 7 to 9 hours or until pork is tender.

■ Skim off any fat from top of cranberry mixture; place roast on cutting board. Slice pork and top with sauce. Serves 6 to 8.

Garlic-Roasted Pork Loin

1 (3 - 4 pound) pork loin
4 teaspoons minced garlic
1 tablespoon ketchup
2 tablespoons soy sauce, divided
2 tablespoons plus ½ cup honey, divided
2 tablespoons rice vinegar

■ Place pork loin on a sheet of foil. Combine
garlic, ketchup, 1 tablespoon soy sauce and
2 tablespoons honey and rub evenly over pork.
Place pork loin in sprayed slow cooker. Cover
and cook on LOW for 7 to 9 hours.

■ Combine remaining soy sauce, remaining
½ cup honey and vinegar in saucepan and
cook until hot, about 10 minutes. Slice
pork diagonally and place on serving platter.
Drizzle sauce over pork slices. Serves 8.

_Cut loss; don't toss. Bits of
leftovers can easily go into soups,
stews, stir-fry, sandwiches, etc., later
in the week._

Fruit-Stuffed Pork Roast

1 (3 - 3½ pound) boneless pork loin roast
1 cup mixed dried fruit
1 tablespoon dried onion flakes
1 teaspoon thyme
½ teaspoon ground cinnamon
2 tablespoons canola oil
½ cup apple cider

Cut horizontally through center of pork
almost to opposite side. Open pork like
a book.

Layer dried fruit and onion flakes in opening.
Bring halves of pork together and tie at 1-inch
intervals with kitchen twine.

Combine ½ teaspoon salt, thyme, cinnamon
and ½ teaspoon pepper in small bowl and rub
into roast. Place roast in skillet with oil and
brown roast on all sides. Place in sprayed slow
cooker and pour apple cider in cooker.

Cover and cook on LOW for 3 to 4 hours.
Let stand for 10 or 15 minutes before slicing.
Serves 6 to 8.

Brown Sugar Glazed Ham

1 (1 pound) cooked smoked ½-inch thick center cut
ham slice
⅓ cup orange juice
⅓ cup packed brown sugar
2 teaspoons dijon-style mustard

▨ Place ham slice in sprayed slow cooker.
Combine juice, brown sugar and mustard in
small bowl. Spread over ham slice.

▨ Cover and cook on LOW for 3 to 4 hours
or until ham has glossy glaze. Cut ham into
individual servings. Serves 4 to 5.

If you have any leftover cooked pasta,
meat or vegetables, use them for soup
ingredients. Most cooked vegetables
can also be pureed and stirred in to
thicken soups.

Cherry Ham Loaf

Great for leftover ham

1½ pounds cooked, ground ham
1 pound ground turkey
2 eggs
1 cup seasoned breadcrumbs
2 teaspoons chicken seasoning

◼ Make foil handles for meat loaf (see page 97).

◼ Combine all ingredients in bowl and mix well.
Shape into short loaf that fits into sprayed oval
slow cooker. Cover and cook on LOW for 4 to
5 hours. Serve with Cherry Sauce.

Cherry Sauce:

1 cup cherry preserves
2 tablespoons cider vinegar
Scant ⅛ teaspoon ground cloves
Scant ⅛ teaspoon ground cinnamon

◼ Place cherry preserves, vinegar, cloves and
cinnamon in saucepan and heat. Serve over
slices of Ham Loaf. Serves 4 to 6.

Ben's Ham and Rice

1 (6.7 ounce) box brown-wild rice, mushroom recipe
3 - 4 cups cooked, chopped or cubed ham
1 (4 ounce) can sliced mushrooms, drained
1 (10 ounce) package frozen green peas
2 cups chopped celery

Combine rice, seasoning packet, ham, mushrooms, peas, and celery plus 2⅔ cups water in sprayed slow cooker. Stir to mix well. Cover and cook on LOW for 2 to 4 hours. Serves 4 to 6.

Delectable Apricot Ribs

4 - 5 pounds baby back pork ribs
1 (16 ounce) jar apricot preserves
⅓ cup soy sauce
¼ cup packed light brown sugar
2 teaspoons garlic powder
¼ cup apple cider vinegar

Place ribs in sprayed slow cooker.

Combine preserves, soy sauce, brown sugar, garlic powder and vinegar in bowl and spoon over ribs. Cover and cook on LOW for 6 to 7 hours. Serves 8 to 10.

Barbecued Ribs

4 - 5 pounds pork spareribs, cut into 2-rib pieces
I cup spicy ketchup
¼ cup vinegar
⅔ cup packed brown sugar
I tablespoon Worcestershire sauce

■ Preheat broiler.

■ Place spareribs on rack in shallow baking pan
and brown for 10 to 15 minutes on each side.
Drain and place in sprayed slow cooker.

■ Combine ketchup, vinegar, brown sugar,
Worcestershire and ½ teaspoon salt in small
bowl. Pour mixture over ribs; turning ribs to
evenly coat.

■ Cover and cook on LOW for 5 to 6 hours or
until ribs are tender. Serves 6.

Mama Mia Meat Loaf

1 (15 ounce) jar spaghetti sauce, divided
1 pound Italian pork sausage, removed from casing
1 pound ground beef
1 cup breadcrumbs
1 cup chopped onion
1 cup grated parmesan cheese
1 teaspoon minced garlic
1 egg

■ Make foil handles for meat loaf (see page 97).

■ Combine ½ cup spaghetti sauce, 1 teaspoon
each of salt and pepper, and all remaining
ingredients in large bowl; mix well. Form into
loaf in sprayed slow cooker.

■ Pour remaining sauce over loaf. Cover and
cook on LOW 5 to 7 hours. Serves 8.

*Have old memories,
but keep young hopes.*

Cheesy Veggie-Crab Casserole

3 tablespoons plus ¼ cup (½ stick) butter, divided
2 ribs celery, thinly sliced
1 (10 ounce) package frozen chopped bell peppers
       and onions, thawed
¼ cup flour
2 (14 ounce) cans chicken broth
1¼ cups instant rice
2 (6 once) cans crabmeat, drained, flaked
1 cup shredded cheddar cheese
1 (4 ounce) can sliced mushrooms, drained
½ cup sliced almonds
1 cup seasoned breadcrumbs

▣ Melt 3 tablespoons butter in skillet on medium
   heat and lightly saute celery and bell peppers
   and onions. Add flour and stir well. Slowly
   add chicken broth, stirring constantly and
   cook until slightly thickened.

▣ Combine rice, crabmeat, cheese, mushrooms
   and almonds in bowl. Stir in sauce and
   transfer to sprayed slow cooker. Cover and
   cook on HIGH for 3 to 5 hours.

▣ Spoon contents of slow cooker into ovenproof
   serving dish. Melt ¼ cup (½ stick) butter
   and combine with breadcrumbs in small bowl;
   sprinkle over contents of serving dish. Place
   under broiler until crumbs are slightly brown.
   Serves 5 to 6.

Super Shrimp and Rice

1 (16 ounce) package frozen salad shrimp, thawed
¾ cup chicken broth
1 red bell pepper, seeded, cut into strips
1 teaspoon chili powder
¼ teaspoon dried oregano
¼ cup (½ stick) butter, melted
1 (10 ounce) package frozen green peas, thawed
¼ cup sun-dried tomatoes, sliced
2 cups cooked rice

▣ Combine shrimp, broth, bell pepper, chili
   powder, oregano and butter in sprayed slow
   cooker. Cover and cook on LOW for 2 hours.

▣ Stir in green peas, tomatoes and rice; cover
   and cook for additional 15 minutes or until
   mixture is thoroughly hot. Serves 4 to 6.

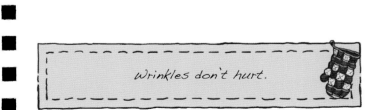

Wrinkles don't hurt.

Yummy Tuna Bake

2 (6 ounce) cans white tuna, drained, flaked
1 (10 ounce) can cream of chicken soup
3 eggs, hard-boiled, chopped
3 ribs celery, thinly sliced
1 red bell pepper, seeded, chopped
½ cup coarsely chopped pecans
½ cup mayonnaise
2 cups crushed potato chips, divided

▣ Combine tuna, soup, eggs, celery, bell
pepper, pecans, mayonnaise, 1 teaspoon
pepper, half potato chips and a little salt
in bowl and mix well.

▣ Transfer to sprayed slow cooker. Cover and
cook on LOW for 5 to 7 hours. When ready
to serve, sprinkle remaining potato chips on
top. Serves 4 to 5.

Because the lid forms a seal with the
slow cooker, there is very little
evaporation of the cooking liquid. If a
stovetop recipe is converted to the slow
cooker method, the amount of liquid used
(water, broth, etc.) should be reduced.
Liquid can be added later if needed.

Desserts

Good-Time Apple Crisp

½ cup flour
1½ cups sugar, divided
½ teaspoon ground cinnamon, divided
¼ cup (½ stick) butter, cut in pieces
½ cup chopped pecans
2 teaspoons lemon juice
¼ teaspoon ground ginger
5 - 6 Granny Smith apples, peeled, cut into wedges
Vanilla ice cream

▢ Combine flour, ½ cup sugar, ¼ teaspoon cinnamon and butter pieces in bowl. Work butter into flour mixture with pastry blender or fork until mixture becomes coarse crumbs. Stir in pecans.

▢ In separate bowl, whisk remaining sugar, remaining cinnamon, lemon juice and ginger. Add apple wedges and toss for mixture to cover apples. Transfer to sprayed slow cooker and sprinkle flour-pecan mixture over apples.

▢ Cover and cook on LOW for 4 hours or on HIGH for 2 hours. Serve warm or at room temperature with a dip of vanilla ice cream. Serves 6 to 8.

Chocolate Party Fondue

Your slow cooker can easily become a fondue pot.

2 (7 ounce) bars chocolate, chopped
1 (4 ounce) bar white chocolate, chopped
1 (7 ounce) jar marshmallow creme
¾ cup half-and-half cream
½ cup slivered almonds, chopped, toasted
¼ cup amaretto liqueur
Pound cake and fruit

▪ Combine chocolate bars, white chocolate bar, marshmallow creme, half-and-half cream and almonds in small, sprayed slow cooker.

▪ Cover and cook on LOW for about 2 hours or until chocolates melt.

▪ Stir to mix well and fold in amaretto liqueur. Cut pound cake into small squares and dip into fondue. Fruits such as strawberries, grapes, slices of apple, pear, kiwi and bananas, just to name a few are great too. Serves 8 to 10.

Blueberry Goodness

1 (20 ounce) can blueberry pie filling
1 (18 ounce) box yellow cake mix
½ cup (1 stick) butter, softened
1 cup chopped walnuts
Vanilla ice cream

■ Place pie filling in sprayed slow cooker.
   Combine cake mix, butter and walnuts and
   spread over pie filling.

■ Cover and cook on LOW for 2 hours. Serve
   over ice cream. Serves 8 to 10.

Once food has been cooked and served,
it is best to remove the food from the
ceramic insert to refrigerate. The liners
of slow cookers are made of very heavy
material and do not cool quickly. This can
enable the growth of harmful bacteria.

Slow Cooker Bananas Foster

5 bananas, sliced
½ cup packed brown sugar
½ cup (1 stick) butter, melted
¼ cup rum, optional
Vanilla ice cream

Mix brown sugar, butter and rum in sprayed
slow cooker. Add banana slices and coat
with brown sugar mixture. Cook on LOW
for 1 hour.

Remove bananas from slow cooker and pour
over individual bowls of ice cream. Serve
immediately. Serves 4.

TIP: If you want Bananas Foster to flame, do not add
rum to slow cooker. After you pour bananas over ice
cream, pour 151-proof rum over bananas. Light the
rum with a match just after you serve it and it will
flame briefly for a nice effect.

Delicious Bread Pudding

8 cups cubed leftover hot rolls, cinnamon rolls
    or bread
2 cups milk
4 large eggs
¾ cup sugar
⅓ cup packed brown sugar
¼ cup (½ stick) butter, melted
1 teaspoon vanilla
¼ teaspoon ground nutmeg
1 cup finely chopped pecans
Frozen whipped topping, thawed

▧ Place cubed bread or rolls in sprayed
    slow cooker.

▧ Combine milk, eggs, sugar, brown sugar,
    butter, vanilla and nutmeg in bowl and beat
    until smooth. Stir in pecans and pour
    over bread.

▧ Cover and cook on LOW for 3 hours. Serve
    with whipped topping. Serves 8.

Slow Chocolate Fix

1 (18 ounce) box chocolate cake mix
1 (8 ounce) carton sour cream
4 eggs, beaten
¾ cup canola oil
1 (3.4 ounce) box instant chocolate pudding mix
¾ cup chopped pecans
Vanilla ice cream

Mix cake mix, sour cream, eggs, oil, pudding mix, pecans and 1 cup water in bowl. Pour into sprayed slow cooker.

Cover and cook on LOW for 6 to 8 hours. Serve warm with vanilla ice cream. Serves 6 to 8.

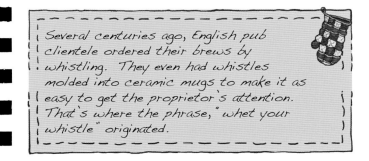

Several centuries ago, English pub clientele ordered their brews by whistling. They even had whistles molded into ceramic mugs to make it as easy to get the proprietor's attention. That's where the phrase, "whet your whistle" originated.

Index

Cookbooks Published by Cookbook Resources, LLC
Bringing Family and Friends to the Table

The Best 1001 Short, Easy Recipes
1001 Slow Cooker Recipes
1001 Short, Easy, Inexpensive Recipes
1001 Fast Easy Recipes
1001 America's Favorite Recipes
Easy Slow Cooker Cookbook
Busy Woman's Slow Cooker Recipes
Busy Woman's Quick & Easy Recipes
365 Easy Soups and Stews
365 Easy Chicken Recipes
365 Easy One-Dish Recipes
365 Easy Soup Recipes
365 Easy Vegetarian Recipes
365 Easy Casserole Recipes
365 Easy Pasta Recipes
365 Easy Slow Cooker Recipes
Super Simple Cupcake Recipes
Leaving Home Cookbook
and Survival Guide
Essential 3-4-5 Ingredient Recipes
Ultimate 4 Ingredient Cookbook
Easy Cooking with 5 Ingredients
The Best of Cooking with 3 Ingredients
Easy Diabetic Recipes
Ultimate 4 Ingredient Diabetic Cookbook
4-Ingredient Recipes for 30-Minute Meals
Cooking with Beer
The Washington Cookbook
The Pennsylvania Cookbook
The California Cookbook
Best-Loved New England Recipes
Best-Loved Canadian Recipes
Best-Loved Recipes
from the Pacific Northwest

Easy Slow Cooker Recipes
(Handbook with Photos)
Cool Smoothies (Handbook with Photos)
Easy Cupcake Recipes
(Handbook with Photos)
Easy Soup Recipes (Handbook with Photos)
Classic Tex-Mex and Texas Cooking
Best-Loved Southern Recipes
Classic Southwest Cooking
Miss Sadie's Southern Cooking
Classic Pennsylvania Dutch Cooking
The Quilters' Cookbook
Healthy Cooking with 4 Ingredients
Trophy Hunter's Wild Game Cookbook
Recipe Keeper
Simple Old-Fashioned Baking
Quick Fixes with Cake Mixes
Kitchen Keepsakes
& More Kitchen Keepsakes
Cookbook 25 Years
Texas Longhorn Cookbook
Gifts for the Cookie Jar
All New Gifts for the Cookie Jar
The Big Bake Sale Cookbook
Easy One-Dish Meals
Easy Potluck Recipes
Easy Casseroles Cookbook
Easy Desserts
Sunday Night Suppers
Easy Church Suppers
365 Easy Meals
Gourmet Cooking with 5 Ingredients
Muffins In A Jar
A Little Taste of Texas
A Little Taste of Texas II
Ultimate Gifts for the Cookie Jar

cookbook
resources LLC

www.cookbookresources.com
Toll free 866-229-2665
Your Ultimate Source for Easy Cookbooks